The Huge Book of Awesome Facts

by
Jake Jacobs

Kindle Edition

* * * * *

Published by Jake Jacobs at Amazon Kindle

1.

Conan's ex-drummer and Slipknot's current drummer are father and son.

Reference: (https://www.youtube.com/watch?v=KW86Vr9Engg)

2.

A man had been suffering from severe headaches, bad breath and breathing difficulties but never knew why. When the symptoms became unbearable, he went to the doctors and they found a 10 centimeter blade in his head that broke off without him realizing, during a robbery incident 4 years prior.

Reference: (http://www.theguardian.com/world/2011/feb/18/china-knife-blade-skull-surgery)

3.

Freestyle canoeing ballets exist.

Reference: (http://youtu.be/SSldR9yOJq8)

4.

Arnold Schwarzenegger had an egg thrown at him at a rally, and supported it as freedom of speech.

Reference: (https://www.youtube.com/watch?v=zw97LIBGbR4)

5.

Jimmy Carter said if he became president, he would release all government UFO information to the public. Once elected, he decided not to due to "national security concerns".

Reference:
(http://en.wikipedia.org/wiki/Jimmy_Carter_UFO_incident#Personal
_impact)

6.

There was a third Apple founder. Ronald Wayne sold his 10% stake
for $800 in 1976.

Reference: (http://mentalfloss.com/article/52275/65-amazing-facts-
will-blow-your-mind)

7.

Jerry West was the first and only player to ever be named NBA
finals MVP from the losing team.

Reference:(https://en.wikipedia.org/wiki/Bill_Russell_NBA_Finals_
Most_Valuable_Player_Award)

8.

In 1982, Key West mayor Dennis Wardlow declared the
independence of his city and seceded from the Union, creating a new
nation known as the "Conch Republic". After a one minute
secession, he surrendered to a naval officer and requested one billion
dollars in "foreign aid."

Reference: (https://en.wikipedia.org/wiki/Florida_Keys)

9.

In the show, "My Name Is Earl", Burt Reynolds was a recurring
guest star and had a son who was played by Norm MacDonald. To
do this, he used his SNL Burt Reynolds impression.

Reference: (http://mynameisearl.wikia.com/wiki/Little_Chubby)

10.

Benjamin Franklin wasn't allowed to write the declaration of Independence because it was feared that he would hide a joke in it.

Reference:
(http://www.history.army.mil/books/RevWar/ss/franklin.htm)

11.

The movie, "Mars Attacks!" was based on a popular trading card series from 1962 that was notorious for its depictions of extreme violence.

Reference: (https://en.wikipedia.org/wiki/Mars_Attacks)

12.

Muhammed Ali's two victories over Sonny Liston, his first world heavyweight championship victory in 1964, and the 1965 rematch, were allegedly fixed. The rematch is especially controversial, with witnesses, fans, and experts on both sides of the debate.

Reference:(https://en.wikipedia.org/wiki/Muhammad_Ali_vs._Sonny_Liston#Was_the_fight_fixed.3F)

13.

In 1990, a British Airways pilot was sucked half way out of the planes window for over 20 minutes. He was only kept in by a crew member holding onto his belt. He survived with frostbite and a broken arm.

Reference:
(https://en.wikipedia.org/wiki/British_Airways_Flight_5390)

14.

Mexico is one of the few countries which has technical capabilities to manufacture nuclear weapons, but has renounced them and pledged to only use its nuclear technology for peaceful purposes, following the Treaty of Tlatelolco in 1968.

Reference:(https://en.wikipedia.org/wiki/Mexico_and_weapons_of_mass_destruction#cite_note-1)

15.

Fox was contractually obligated to offer Frank Sinatra the role of John McClane in Die Hard.

Reference: (https://en.wikipedia.org/wiki/Die_Hard)

16.

The Japji hymn by Guru Nanak is considered to be the key to Sri Guru Granth Sahib and an epitome of the Sikh doctrine. It appears as the first poem in Sri Guru Granth Sahib. Japji lays stress on the brotherhood of the human race.

Reference: (https://www.youtube.com/watch?v=td28WMtKgCc)

17.

The Milky Way and Andromeda galaxies will collide in about 4 billion years; being nicknamed Milkomeda.

Reference:
(https://en.wikipedia.org/wiki/Andromeda%E2%80%93Milky_Way_collision)

18.

The G spot is named after German gynecologist Ernst Gräfenberg.

Reference: (https://en.wikipedia.org/wiki/G-spot)

19.

Out of the thirty couples from "The Bachelor" and "The Bachelorette," five of them are still together.

Reference: (http://www.wetpaint.com/how-many-official-bachelor-and-bachelorette-couples-actually-make-it-638094/)

20.

The metallic smell of blood and coins is due to the oils in your skin decomposing on the iron in the blood or coins.

Reference: (http://www.livescience.com/4233-coins-smell.html?til)

21.

In an attempt to make sense of African civilizations and art, one archeologist proposed a theory on how an ancient colony of white Greeks must've lived there long before Europe came into contact with Africa.

Reference:
(https://en.wikipedia.org/wiki/Bronze_Head_from_Ife#Impact_on_art_history)

22.

The mosquito is actually a very weak flier. The American Mosquito Control Association says just a fan can keep them away.

Reference: (http://www.nytimes.com/2013/07/16/science/a-low-tech-mosquito-deterrent.html)

23.

Bubbles from a bubble bath thermally insulate the surface of the water, keeping the bath warm for a longer period of time.

Reference:
(http://www.thenakedscientists.com/HTML/questions/qotw/question/3111/)

24.

The runner's high is now thought to be a product of endocannabinoids, which are your body's version of the THC found in marijuana, and not endorphins, which are your body's opioids. Endorphins are too large to pass the blood-brain border, and mice bred without cannabinoid receptors don't enjoy running.

Reference: (http://well.blogs.nytimes.com/2011/02/16/phys-ed-what-really-causes-runners-high/?_r=0)

25.

A baseball player only needs to spend one day in the major leagues to earn free healthcare for life.

Reference: (http://www.thestreet.com/story/10983698/1/even-pro-athletes-worry-about-retirement.html)

26.

By 1974, mainland Britain saw an average of one attack by the IRA, successful or otherwise, every three days.

Reference:
(https://en.wikipedia.org/wiki/Birmingham_pub_bombings)

27.

Vasili Alexandrovich Arkhipov prevented a Russian submarine from launching a nuclear missile at U.S. war ships during the Cuban Missile Crisis, effectively saving the world from nuclear war.

Reference:
(http://phenomena.nationalgeographic.com/2016/03/25/you-and-almost-everyone-you-know-owe-your-life-to-this-man/?utm_source=Facebook&utm_medium=Social&utm_content=link_fb20160606ph-krulwichman&utm_campaign=Content&sf28097536=1)

28.

The current whereabouts of the second most prolific serial killer after 1900 is unknown.

Reference:
(https://en.wikipedia.org/wiki/List_of_serial_killers_by_number_of_victims)

29.

Jason Segel's mother cried in the theatre when she saw her son's nude scene in "Forgetting Sarah Marshall." She then sent a mass e-mail to the rest of her family to warn them about the scene, but stated that it was "essential to the plot."

Reference: (http://www.huffingtonpost.com/2014/06/17/jason-segel-mother_n_5502988.html)

30.

Guinness brewery supported all of its employees who chose to fight in World War I. They were paid half of their wages while away, and their jobs were guaranteed upon their return. The brewery also sent them care packages containing chocolate and condensed milk.

Reference: (http://www.bbc.co.uk/programmes/p01s8vf3)

31.

Eritrea has the worst Freedom of Press in the world; worse than North Korea.

Reference: (https://rsf.org/en/eritrea)

32.

In 1978, D.C. comics published Superman vs. Muhammad Ali.

Reference:
(https://en.wikipedia.org/wiki/Superman_vs._Muhammad_Ali)

33.

Will Smith publicly defends the Church of Scientology and the story of the movie "After Earth" shows parallels to the book "Dianetics" written by Ron Hubbard.

Reference:
(https://en.wikipedia.org/wiki/After_Earth#Controversies)

34.

Winston Churchill got hit by a car and almost died while in the United States, after not looking both ways before crossing the road.

Reference:
(http://www.nytimes.com/2006/05/07/nyregion/thecity/07fyi.html)

35.

An art professor from Syracuse University created a single tree that bears 40 different types of fruit after learning that an orchard full of 150 - 200 year old native fruit trees was going to be destroyed.

Reference: (http://abcnews.go.com/Lifestyle/pretty-tree-grows-40-kinds-fruit/story?id=24702111)

36.

There is a man indigenous to Brazil that is believed to be the last of his tribe. He is known as the Man of the Hole.

Reference: (https://en.wikipedia.org/wiki/Man_of_the_Hole)

37.

TWA Flight 541 was hijacked in 1978 by the daughter of a woman who was killed while hijacking a helicopter to free a federal prisoner, who was in prison for hijacking a TWA flight in 1972.

Reference: (https://en.wikipedia.org/wiki/TWA_Flight_541)

38.

The only person to smoke out Snoop Dogg was Willy Nelson.

Reference:
(https://www.youtube.com/watch?v=e79J0uiFIG4&feature=youtu.be
)

39.

Cashews grow on a tree.

Reference: (http://www.huffingtonpost.com/entry/how-do-cashews-grow_us_56e71e8fe4b065e2e3d6f187?)

40.

When the members of Steely Dan found out that the plot of "You, Me and Dupree," was stolen from one of their songs, they wrote a letter demanding that Owen Wilson come to one of their concerts and apologize onstage or they would have one of their roadies beat him up.

Reference: (http://www.steelydan.com/heyluke.html)

41.

The most successful animal on Earth, in terms of weight, is either the cow or the Antarctic krill. Their DNA has made more copies of itself than any other known gene sequence.

Reference:
(https://en.wikipedia.org/wiki/Biomass_%28ecology%29)

42.

Alligators have five toes on their front legs and four toes on their hind legs.

Reference:(https://nationalzoo.si.edu/Animals/ReptilesAmphibians/Facts/FactSheets/Americanalligator.cfm)

43.

Fist bumps have been scientifically proven to be a safer and more hygienic greeting than handshakes and high-fives.

Reference:(http://www.apic.org/Resource_/TinyMceFileManager/Fist_bump_article_AJIC_August_2014.pdf)

44.

Mimic Octopus can not only change colors, but will also mimic the shapes of other animals, like the flounder, lionfish and sea snakes.

Reference: (https://en.wikipedia.org/wiki/Mimic_octopus)

45.

The longest straight line you could sail on Earth reaches from Pakistan to Russia and is about 20,000 miles.

Reference: (http://observationdeck.kinja.com/the-longest-straight-line-you-can-sail-on-earth-reaches-1136121429)

46.

In Turkey, it's a felony to insult the Turkish Government or any official serving in the Turkish government.

Reference:
(https://en.wikipedia.org/wiki/Article_301_(Turkish_Penal_Code))

47.

During the Peloponnesian War, Athens decided to attack Melos, a small island, neutral to the war. They killed and enslaved everyone and repopulated the island with Athenian citizens. Their excuse was simply that according to the natural law the weak must always be ruled by their superiors.

Reference:(http://www.perseus.tufts.edu/hopper/text?doc=Perseus%3Atext%3A1999.04.0009%3Achapter%3D12%3Asection%3D1%3Asubsection%3D11)

48.

James Otis, a patriot of the American Revolution, told his sister that he hoped when he died he went out like a flash of lightning. He died in 1783 from being struck by lightning.

Reference: (https://en.wikipedia.org/wiki/James_Otis_Jr.)

49.

Police can lawfully search your phone as long as it's encrypted.

Reference: (http://www.howtogeek.com/141953/how-to-encrypt-your-android-phone-and-why-you-might-want-to/)

50.

North Korea revalued its currency in 2009. Citizens were given a week to exchange old money for new, and were only permitted to exchange a certain amount of currency, worth about $120 at the time. This completely wiped out the savings of many families.

Reference:
(http://en.wikipedia.org/wiki/North_Korean_won#Dollar_peg_removed)

51.

Divers in 1900 discovered an Ancient Greek shipwreck with an odd-looking bronze device on board. The device was later determined to be the world's oldest analog computer, dating back to the 1st century B.C.E., thousands of years before similar technologies would be re-discovered.

Reference: (http://polyrad.info/antikythera-mechanism-ancient-greek-shipwreck-analog-computer/)

52.

Acetaminophen and Paracetamol's painkiller and anti-anxiety effects are because it enhances natural cannabinoids' action in the brain.

Reference: (http://www.ncbi.nlm.nih.gov/pubmed/16438952)

53.

Louisiana was the last state in the U.S. to raise the minimum drinking age from 18 to 21 in 1996, doing so only because the Federal Government threatened to revoke $17 million in Federal Highway money if the state didn't comply with the National Minimum Drinking Age Act of 1986.

Reference: (http://www.nytimes.com/1996/07/03/us/louisiana-court-upholds-drinking-age-of-21.html)

54.

Cajuns are an ethnic group that mainly lives in the U.S. state of Louisiana. They consist of the descendants of Acadian exiles, which were French-speakers from Acadia in what are now the Maritimes of Eastern Canada.

Reference: (https://en.wikipedia.org/wiki/Cajuns)

55.

Italy's Credem Bank takes Parmesan cheese from local producers in exchange for cheap loans (charging 3-5% interest, depending on quality) & a fee ensuring the cheese matures properly (2yrs) in the bank vault (cheese is sold if the loan defaults). 430,000 Parmesan wheels ($200M+) are stored there.

Reference: (http://edition.cnn.com/2013/08/15/business/parmesan-cheese-bank-mpe/)

56.

Limes don't float.

Reference:
(http://weirdsciencekids.com/floatinglemonssinkinglimes.html)

57.

Most people in Europe do not use air conditioning.

Reference:
(https://www.washingtonpost.com/news/worldviews/wp/2015/07/22/europe-to-america-your-love-of-air-conditioning-is-stupid/)

58.

The longest video game marathon documented was 138 hours and 34 seconds long, playing Just Dance 2015.

Reference: (http://www.guinnessworldrecords.com/world-records/longest-video-games-marathon/)

59.

Bob Crane, the star of Hogan's Heroes, was found bludgeoned to death with an electric cord tied around his neck. The murder remains officially unsolved, but is thought to relate to his prolific sex life and habit of making secret sex tapes.

Reference: (https://en.wikipedia.org/wiki/Bob_Crane)

60.

A baby born to Ugandan mother during a flight from Amsterdam to Boston became Canadian after born in their airspace.

Reference: (http://news.bbc.co.uk/2/hi/americas/7807001.stm)

61.

The U.S. hasn't been hit by a major hurricane since 2005, the longest "hurricane drought" in recorded history.

Reference: (http://www.livescience.com/50704-hurricane-drought.html)

62.

Pogs were used by the army as currency overseas, because they weigh less than metal coinage.

Reference:
(https://en.wikipedia.org/wiki/Milk_caps_%28game%29#Military_uses)

63.

The FBI has an art crime team composed of 16 special agents dedicated to recovering stolen works of art.

Reference: (https://www.fbi.gov/about-us/investigate/vc_majorthefts/arttheft/art-crime-team)

64.

In 2015, an Air Dubai flight took small arms fire while on approach to Baghdad International Airport.

Reference: (https://en.wikipedia.org/wiki/Flydubai)

65.

40,000 people in Iran rely on a 45KM long "qanat", which is an underground aqueduct, built nearly 3,000 years ago.

Reference: (https://en.wikipedia.org/wiki/Qanat)

66.

The Tupolev TU-144 was Russia's Concorde that met its end at the Paris Airshow, 1973.

Reference: (http://www.tu144sst.com/)

67.

Final Fantasy: The Spirits Within cost $137 million to make, which was $22 million more than Star Wars: The Phantom Menace.

Reference:
(https://en.wikipedia.org/wiki/Final_Fantasy:_The_Spirits_Within)

68.

When FIFA wanted to print the Saudi flag on a football, Saudi officials protested, as it would be "inappropriate" to kick against the Qu'ran verse featured on the flag.

Reference:
(https://en.wikipedia.org/wiki/Flag_of_Saudi_Arabia#History)

69.

The brand "Frigidaire" was so well known in the refrigeration field in the early to mid-1990s that many Americans called any refrigerator a Frigidaire. The name Frigidaire or its antecedent Frigerator may be the origin of the widely-used U.S. slang term "fridge."

Reference: (https://en.wikipedia.org/wiki/Frigidaire)

70.

The United States has killed 20 to 30 million people since World War II.

Reference: (http://www.countercurrents.org/lucas240407.htm)

71.

Hitler didn't like the word "Blitzkrieg" and even said, "I have never used the word Blitzkrieg, because it is a very silly word".

Reference:
(https://en.wikipedia.org/wiki/Blitzkrieg#Origin_of_the_term)

72.

In the 1980s, German AI pioneer Ernst Dickmanns refurbished a Mercedes-Benz van to take input from various cameras and sensors, process it, and guide the navigation of the car. The 5-ton Mercedes traveled hundreds of miles across Germany using autonomous technology, all without a driver.

Reference: (http://www.snapmunk.com/google-now-has-to-make-its-autonomous-cars-more-like-us-dumber-and-more-dangerous/)

73.

Actor Adam Driver is a former Marine and created the "Arts in the Armed Forces", a non-profit organization that brings theatre to the military.

Reference:
(https://www.ted.com/talks/adam_driver_why_i_bring_theater_to_the_military)

74.

Ginger is served with sushi so it can used as a palette cleanser.

Reference: (http://www.ponderweasel.com/why-is-ginger-served-with-sushi/)

75.

There are still unexplored passageways in the Great Pyramid of Giza in Egypt.

Reference: (http://emhotep.net/2012/03/07/locations/lower-egypt/giza-plateau-lower-egypt/the-djedi-project-the-next-generation-in-robotic-archaeology/)

76.

Italian names for pasta usually end in the letter I or E as they are the masculine and feminine pluralizations, singulars normally end in an O such as "Spaghetto", "Raviolo", and "Tortellino".

Reference: (https://en.wikipedia.org/wiki/List_of_pasta)

77.

The smallest shark in the world is the dwarf lantern shark, which is about 8 inches long.

Reference: (https://en.wikipedia.org/wiki/Dwarf_lanternshark)

78.

A Dragon Ball Z special episode had 7 songs of Dream Theater.

Reference:
(https://en.wikipedia.org/wiki/Dragon_Ball_Z:_The_History_of_Trunks#Music)

79.

The Japanese school year is 240 days long, giving their students three more years of total instruction received compared to an American High School grad.

Reference:
(http://www.theatlantic.com/education/archive/2013/10/the-myth-of-im-bad-at-math/280914/?utm_source=SFFB)

80.

There's an entire subculture convinced that people shift around between "alternate realities" to explain why they remember things that didn't happen.

Reference: (http://mandelaeffect.com/about)

81.

There is a genus of spiders called Orsonwelles that are native to the Hawaiian Islands, named in honor of Orson Welles.

Reference: (https://en.wikipedia.org/wiki/Orsonwelles)

82.

In the 1994 Caribbean Cup, due to an unusual variant of the golden goal rule where a goal in extra time was worth double points, Barbados scored an own goal deliberately as it was the only way for them to progress to the finals.

Reference:(https://en.wikipedia.org/wiki/Barbados_4%E2%80%932 _Grenada_%281994_Caribbean_Cup_qualification%29)

83.

There's a road in Yellowknife, Northwest Territories, that is named "Ragged Ass".

Reference:
(https://en.wikipedia.org/wiki/Ragged_Ass_Road_(street))

84.

Napoleon II used a magician to help suppress a rebellion in Algeria by proving French magic was superior to Algerian magic. Robert-Houdin gained the fear and allegiance of the Algerians by catching bullets in his teeth and draining a man's strength by making objects immovable with magnets.

Reference:
(https://partners.nytimes.com/library/magazine/millennium/m1/teller .html)

85.

A real estate broker in the city of Ermelo in the Netherlands found a great way to encourage prospective buyers to take a quick tour of the house that he was selling; his company built a roller coaster through it.

Reference: (https://www.youtube.com/watch?v=D2QOtnLdnLQ)

86.

Frasier and Darth Vader's accents weren't British but in fact Mid-Atlantic, a dialect of American English created by American upper class in the early 20th century.

Reference: (https://en.wikipedia.org/wiki/Mid-Atlantic_accent)

87.

The oldest brewery in the world, the Weihenstephan Brewery, has been in operation since 1040.

Reference:(https://en.wikipedia.org/wiki/Weihenstephan_Abbey#The_world.27s_oldest_continuously_operating_brewery)

88.

The creator of Netflix started the service in the 1990's after being charged $40 for a late Blockbuster rental.

Reference: (http://fortune.com/netflix-versus-hollywood/)

89.

The McRib is available as a permanent menu item in Germany.

Reference: (https://en.wikipedia.org/wiki/McRib)

90.

There's a shade of blue that doesn't reproduce on a black and white copy machine or grayscale scan. It's used extensively in the graphic design industry.

Reference: (https://en.wikipedia.org/wiki/Non-photo_blue)

91.

Peanuts grow underground.

Reference: (http://nationalpeanutboard.org/peanut-info/how-peanuts-grow.htm)

92.

"Vulture funds" make 300% to 2000% profit by buying up debt from heavily indebted poor countries. They sometimes claim up to 13% of GDP in repayments.

Reference: (http://www.afdb.org/en/topics-and-sectors/initiatives-partnerships/african-legal-support-facility/vulture-funds-in-the-sovereign-debt-context/)

93.

Some countries outside of the U.S. have a different brand of Tuong Ot Sriracha than Huy Fong Foods' "Rooster" Tuong Ot Sriracha.

Reference: (http://www.amoeba.com/blog/2013/06/eric-s-blog/sriracha-101-dispelling-myths-and-misinformation-about-sriracha-.html)

94.

Cats sleep an average of two thirds of their lives. This would mean that a 9 year old cat has only been awake for 3 years.

Reference: (http://www.susandaffron.com/how-much-do-cats-sleep/)

95.

Most civilian aircraft are fitted with static discharges or static wicks which are long thin extensions fitted to the trailing end of an airplane's wings or stabilizers. These wicks serve to dissipate precipitation static and help eliminate audio disturbances.

Reference: (http://www.flyingmag.com/technique/tip-week/check-your-wicks)

96.

Woodlice do not urinate.

Reference: (http://www.porcellio.scaber.org/woodlice/wliceod.htm)

97.

Wild ferrets are endangered.

Reference: (https://www.youtube.com/watch?v=pS1tcdDdV8c)

98.

There is a golf course between the two active runways at Bangkok's Don Mueang international airport.

Reference: (https://www.youtube.com/watch?v=dUaBJbDJppQ)

99.

Police sketches of suspects are rarely accurate and researchers have developed software that allows victims to generate a far more realistic representation of the suspect.

Reference:(https://www.youtube.com/watch?v=h81SuD2pltM&feature=youtu.be&list=PLJ8cMiYb3G5eNMPb_MTRyLDzm_AOIk7UF)

100.

When asked what was the greatest political fact of modern times, Otto Von Bismarck, the man behind the unification of Germany, responded that it was, "the inherited and permanent fact that North America speaks English."

Reference:
(http://en.wikiquote.org/wiki/Otto_von_Bismarck#Quotes)

101.

The world's tallest building was supposed to be called The Burj Dubai, but when they ran out of money, the Sheik of Dubai had to ask his big brother to bail them out. The big brother, known as Khalifa bin Zayed Al Nahyan obliged, but they had to name the building The Burj Khalifa.

Reference: (http://www.theaustralian.com.au/news/world/dubais-humiliating-name-change-for-worlds-tallest-building/story-e6frg6so-1225816358890)

102.

Opossum's are the only marsupial found in North America. From eating snakes, they possess a resistant to rattlesnake, cottonmouth and pit viper venom.

Reference: (http://news.nationalgeographic.com/2015/03/150323-opossums-snakes-snakebites-venom-health-world-science/)

103.

One of the Congressmen who set up the House Committee on Un-American Activities was selling falsified passports to the Soviets and offered to spy for them.

Reference:
(https://en.wikipedia.org/wiki/Samuel_Dickstein_(congressman))

104.

John Gordon was the last person executed by Rhode Island. During his trial, the instructions to the jury were, "to give greater weight to Yankee witnesses than Irish witnesses." Mr. Gordon was posthumously pardoned in 2011.

Reference:
(https://en.wikipedia.org/wiki/John_Gordon_(Rhode_Island))

105.

A 13 year old girl from Louisiana is working to be a crew member on a Mars One.

Reference: (http://www.mars-one.com/about-mars-one/ambassadors/alyssa-carson)

106.

When Armenia and Azerbaijan reached an agreement concerning the Karabakh issue, a group of 5 armed men stormed the Armenian parliament and killed the Armenian Prime Minister and 7 others.

Reference:
(https://en.wikipedia.org/wiki/Armenian_parliament_shooting)

107.

Only four presidents have visited all 50 states whilst in office.

Reference: (https://www.washingtonpost.com/news/post-politics/wp/2015/05/07/only-three-presidents-have-visited-all-50-states-in-office-until-now/)

108.

Illusionist Harry Houdini was falsely reported as taking part of the first aerial flight in Australia and a century later, some major news outlets still credit him with this feat.

Reference:
(https://en.wikipedia.org/wiki/Harry_Houdini#Falsely_reported_as_pioneer)

109.

Over 250 cinemas in the United Kingdom have Autism Friendly Screenings in which the volume is lower, the lighting is darker and you can take your own food and drink.

Reference: (https://www.dimensions-uk.org/families/autism-friendly-screenings/)

110.

Starting in the 1960s, the American Heart Association advised the public to eat less saturated fat and switch to vegetable oils for a "healthy heart". The American Heart Association was founded in part by the makers of Crisco.

Reference:
(http://www.wsj.com/articles/SB10001424052702303678404579533760760481486)

111.

Despite their widespread prevalence, there have not been any new establishments of Aspen Seedlings in the Western USA in 10,000 years due to the climate having changed so drastically. All existing Western Aspens are those which germinated 10,000 years ago.

Reference: (https://en.wikipedia.org/wiki/Pando_(tree)???)

112.

There are a set of episodes from Mister Roger's Neighborhood that were banned for depictions of nuclear war.

Reference: (http://lostmedia.wikia.com/wiki/Mister_Roger's_Neighborhood:_%22Conflict%22_%281983_TV_episodes%29)

113.

"Frasier" had a number of major celebrities call in to his show. The credits on the season finale listed those celebrities who called in that season.

Reference: (https://www.youtube.com/watch?v=dNPrlVXeuEA)

114.

On the border between the U.S. and Canada, there is a 5,500 mile long, 20 foot wide "no touching zone" that is kept totally clear of trees.

Reference:
(https://www.youtube.com/watch?v=qMkYlIA7mgw&feature=youtu.be)

115.

Salt is iodized because it is the simplest and most cost-effective measure available to battle iodine deficiency, which is the leading preventable cause of intellectual and developmental disabilities.

Reference: (https://en.wikipedia.org/wiki/Iodised_salt)

116.

If early deep sea divers encountered a catastrophic airline failure, the massive decompression would literally "squeeze" all their soft tissue into their helmets.

Reference: (https://www.youtube.com/watch?v=LEY3fN4N3D8)

117.

There is a word in the Swedish Dictionary named after Zlatan Ibrahimović, "Zlatanera" meaning "to dominate".

Reference: (http://uk.reuters.com/article/uk-soccer-sweden-ibrahimovic-idUKBRE8BR0G620121228)

118.

Juan translates to John in English.

Reference: (https://en.wikipedia.org/wiki/Juan)

119.

Since 1981, Mexico doesn't extradite to countries that are seeking the death penalty, and has successfully defended 400 of its citizens charged with a capital offence in the United States.

Reference:(https://en.wikipedia.org/wiki/Capital_punishment_in_Mexico#International_relations)

120.

Red kidney beans are poisonous if they're not prepared properly. As few as 5 beans can make you seriously sick. Cooking them in a Crockpot can make the beans more poisonous than not cooking them at all.

Reference:
(http://www.foodreference.com/html/artredkidneybeanpoisoning.html)

121.

The Sentinelese tribe survived a tsunami in 2004. They lack the knowledge to make fire and are regarded as living in the Stone Age.

Reference: (https://en.wikipedia.org/wiki/Sentinelese_people)

122.

During the official opening of the Sydney Harbor Bridge in 1932, a man on horseback cut the ribbon with his sword, upstaging the senior politician who was supposed to cut it.

Reference: (https://www.youtube.com/watch?v=19R0d1VCGxM)

123.

There is a code representing the Klingon language in an official international system for language identification.

Reference: (http://www.loc.gov/standards/iso639-2/php/English_list.php)

124.

Victor Wong, Egg from "Big Trouble in Little China", died as a result of exhaustion due to staying up and watching the wall to wall coverage of the September 11th attacks.

Reference:
(https://en.wikipedia.org/wiki/Victor_Wong_%28actor_born_1927%29#Death)

125.

Bill Shepherd, the first U.S. Navy SEAL that became a NASA Astronaut and first commander of the ISS, was asked what he does best in his astronaut candidate interview. He answered, "kill people with a knife."

Reference: (http://www.space.com/2322-nasa-space-shuttle-cheers-25-years-veteran-space-reporter.html)

126.

The actor for Saruman in Lord of The Rings is a direct descendant of Charlemagne and shares his coat of arms. He also made a heavy metal single about him.

Reference: (http://www.aux.tv/2011/04/this-exists-sir-christopher-lees-heavy-metal-career/)

127.

Emperor Houfei of the Liu Song Dynasty was deposed by one of his generals after he was so intrigued by the size of said general's belly that he had a target painted on it and fired blunt arrows at it.

Reference:
(https://en.wikipedia.org/wiki/Latter_Deposed_Emperor_of_Liu_So
ng#Reign)

128.

North Korea has their own internet service.

Reference: (https://en.wikipedia.org/wiki/Kwangmyong_(network))

129.

King Ferdinand VII of Spain married two of his nieces.

Reference:
(https://en.wikipedia.org/wiki/Ferdinand_VII_of_Spain#Marriages)

130.

Sony has a patent on making viewers yell product names out loud to end TV ads.

Reference: (http://www.fastcodesign.com/1670640/sony-files-patent-to-make-tv-ads-into-video-games)

131.

Hong Kong is not a city in the People's Republic of China. Hong Kong has autonomy, its own currency and flag.

Reference:(https://en.wikipedia.org/w/index.php?title=Hong_Kong&mobileaction=toggle_view_desktop)

132.

The Russians sent and returned the first animals to the moon in 1968. The animals were tortoises.

Reference: (http://www.animalplanet.com/tv-shows/call-of-the-wildman/lists/9-tortoises-orbited-the-moon-before-astronauts-did/)

133.

The movie Madagascar references over 50 scenes and characters from other movies.

Reference: (http://madagascar.wikia.com/wiki/Movie_References-Parodies)

134.

Franklin D. Roosevelt was the first sitting president to fly.

Reference: (http://www.airspacemag.com/daily-planet/the-first-presidential-flight-2901615/?no-ist)

135.

An ultra-light craft, like paper airplane, could in theory be dropped from space and land safely on Earth. There have even been discussion about releasing one from the International Space Station to see what would happen.

Reference: (http://www.newscientist.com/article/dn13208-origami-spaceplane-aims-for-space-station-descent.html#.VLYPqSvF98G)

136.

Texas Instruments produces, designs, and manufactures military weapons such as missiles and bombs, including the world's first laser-guided bomb, known as the BOLT-117.

Reference:
(https://en.wikipedia.org/wiki/Texas_Instruments#Missiles_and_laser-guided_bombs)

137.

Most if not all of the universe can be mathematically modeled in 2 dimensions, implying that we perceive our reality as something like a hologram.

Reference: (https://en.wikipedia.org/wiki/Holographic_principle)

138.

There are more second-language speakers of English than native speakers.

Reference:
(https://www.youtube.com/watch?v=jdSiFKo8Ny4&feature=youtu.be)

139.

Feed sacks became fashionable to wear after the dust bowl. Manufacturers started turning out bags with colorful designs to help boost sales.

Reference:
(http://americanhistory.si.edu/collections/search/object/nmah_1105750)

140.

Dr. Seuss was a strong supporter of Japanese internment. He also drew a racist, anti-Japanese cartoon throughout World War II.

Reference: (http://www.tofugu.com/2013/02/20/dr-seuss/)

141.

The CIA funded the Dalai Lama $1.7 million a year in the 1960s to launch guerrilla operations against the Chinese regime.

Reference:
(https://simple.wikipedia.org/wiki/Dalai_Lama#Modern_history)

142.

Venus rotates 256 times slower than Earth and is one of two plants that rotate retrograde.

Reference:(https://en.wikipedia.org/w/index.php?title=Venus&mobil eaction=toggle_view_desktop)

143.

Prince Harry's name is actually Prince Henry.

Reference: (https://en.wikipedia.org/wiki/Prince_Harry)

144.

A professor proposed a policy of automatic retaliation that would serve to end rocket attacks on Israel. If a rocket was fired at Israel, an automated missile would fire at an arbitrary spot in Gaza without human input, meaning if militants rocketed Israel, they would also be rocketing themselves.

Reference:
(https://en.wikipedia.org/wiki/Dahiya_doctrine#Similar_suggestions
)

145.

Adolf Hitler's primary physician recorded Hitler's sex as homosexual and as taking female hormones.

Reference: (http://www.breitbart.com/national-security/2013/05/09/new-evidence-from-his-doctors-shows-hitler-was-gay/)

146.

Peter Dinklage is the only American cast member in Game of Thrones with a leading role.

Reference:
(http://virtuallinguist.typepad.com/the_virtual_linguist/2012/03/british-accents-in-game-of-thrones.html)

147.

As of 2015, 52 percent of businesswomen in the United States were once Girl Scouts.

Reference: (https://www.girlscouts.org/content/dam/girlscouts-gsusa/forms-and-documents/about-girl-scouts/research/gs-alumnae-by-the-numbers.pdf)

148.

A roundabout is called a "kipilefti" in Swahili.

Reference: (http://blogjam.name/?p=10228)

149.

80% of Bitcoin mining takes place in China.

Reference: (http://dcebrief.com/does-chinas-control-over-bitcoin-mining-threaten-bitcoin/)

150.

Even in today's sitcoms, a large percentage of the people in the laugh track have since passed away. Meaning that we watch comedies marked by the laughter of dead people.

Reference: (http://www.tvparty.com/laugh.html)

151.

The headquarters of MasterCard are located at Purchase, New York.

Reference: (https://www.mastercard.us/en-us/about-mastercard/who-we-are/global-locations.html)

152.

The Chicago Police Department has a network of cameras installed, both public and privately owned called POD's, which can be accessed and controlled by officers at any given time without a warrant.

Reference: (http://home.chicagopolice.org/inside-the-cpd/pod-program/)

153.

Comedy Central is the result of two TV channels merging in 1991, one of the channels belonging to MTV.

Reference: (http://logos.wikia.com/wiki/Comedy_Central)

154.

Hindustan Ambassador is one of the longest running production cars, its design having stayed the same from the late 1950s up to its demise in 2014.

Reference: (https://en.wikipedia.org/wiki/Hindustan_Ambassador)

155.

John Belushi would sabotage anything written by women when he was on SNL, because he believed women were 'fundamentally not funny'.

Reference: (http://www.huffingtonpost.com/2011/04/13/john-belushi-sexist-jane-curtain_n_848646.html)

156.

Rapper Obie Trice was shot in the back of his head while driving, and remained driving until he found the police. The bullet was never removed from his head.

Reference: (http://articles.chicagotribune.com/2006-08-17/features/0608170302_1_lodge-freeway-bullet-range-rover)

157.

There is no concept of an "Alpha" Wolf in the wild and a wolf pack is nothing but two parents along with their younger cubs.

Reference: (http://io9.gizmodo.com/why-everything-you-know-about-wolf-packs-is-wrong-502754629)

158.

George Wallace ran as a third party candidate in 1968, won 46 electoral votes, and was the last third party candidate to carry a state.

Reference: (https://en.wikipedia.org/wiki/George_Wallace)

159.

The longest sniper kill is at 1.5 miles.

Reference:
(https://www.youtube.com/watch?v=wVHEHgnOSOI&feature=youtu.be)

160.

There is a library that was built on the U.S. / Canadian border. Exiting the library through the opposite entrance requires one to report to the country's customs thereafter.

Reference:
(http://en.wikipedia.org/wiki/Haskell_Free_Library_and_Opera_House)

161.

A maintenance worker once dropped a socket on a nuclear missile, piercing its shell and causing an explosion that launched the warhead.

Reference: (http://www.ucsusa.org/content-block/bad-repair-day?id=8985)

162.

An irrational number raised to the power of an irrational number can be rational.

Reference:
(https://www.youtube.com/watch?v=VCaj1lU3kow&feature=youtu.be)

163.

Wirth's Law states that software is getting slower more rapidly than hardware is getting faster.

Reference: (https://en.wikipedia.org/wiki/Wirth%27s_law)

164.

The United States' nuclear arsenal still runs off 8 inch floppy disks.

Reference: (http://motherboard.vice.com/read/americas-nuclear-arsenal-still-runs-off-floppy-disks)

165.

In the 19th century, sunglasses were being worn by those suffering from syphilis. This was because sensitivity to light is a symptom of the STD.

Reference: (http://www.racked.com/2015/4/6/8349545/sunglasses-history)

166.

Napoleon may have had horrible hemorrhoids during the battle of Waterloo, which prevented him from riding on his horse and surveying the battlefield; therefore, losing the pivotal battle.

Reference: (http://www.history.com/news/7-things-you-may-not-know-about-the-battle-of-waterloo)

167.

The first public use of glow sticks was at a 1971 Grateful Dead show.

Reference: (https://thump.vice.com/en_us/article/the-guy-who-invented-glow-sticks-had-no-idea-they-were-so-popular)

168.

In Jordan, entire families can be exiled from their homes and jobs if a relative murders someone. This is done to prevent a cycle of revenge killings, because the family of the victim is given the legal right to kill members of the murderer's family.

Reference: (http://www.jordantimes.com/news/local/eviction-entire-clan-murder-suspect-outrageous-violation-human-rights%E2%80%99)

169.

The Disney character, "Goofy," was originally named Dippy Dawg. He first appeared in Mickey's Revue in 1932 and by his seventh appearance in Orphan's Benefit in 1934, he gained the new name, Goofy, and became a regular member of the group.

Reference: (http://disney.wikia.com/wiki/Goofy#Early_years)

170.

Microsoft Sued the creators Lindows, a Linux distro designed to be compatible with Windows, only to end up paying them $20 million for the trademark rights.

Reference: (https://en.wikipedia.org/wiki/Microsoft_Corp._v._Lindows.com,_Inc.)

171.

There is a condition in which you think you hear a loud bang as you fall asleep when there's really nothing there. More unsettling than that is the name, Exploding Head Syndrome.

Reference: (http://en.wikipedia.org/wiki/Exploding_head_syndrome)

172.

Parking meters do not have to be paid on Sunday in New York City.

Reference: (http://www.nyc.gov/html/dot/html/motorist/parking-rates.shtml)

173.

The founder of Tim Horton's died as a result of drunk driving in 1974. His business partner offered his wife $1 million for her stake in the company, which had 40 stores at the time, and she accepted. He then went on to grow the chain into 4,600 stores by 2013.

Reference: (https://en.wikipedia.org/wiki/Tim_Horton)

174.

Brett Farve and Payton Manning are currently the only NFL Quarterbacks that have beaten all 32 teams.

Reference: (http://www.cbssports.com/nfl/eye-on-football/24700614/peyton-manning-is-second-qb-to-beat-all-32-teams-after-win-over-colts)

175.

Dolly, the famous cloned sheep, was named after Dolly Parton, because the sheep's DNA was derived from a mammary gland.

Reference: (https://en.wikipedia.org/wiki/Dolly_%28sheep%29)

176.

The phrase "whet your appetite" has nothing to do with your mouth watering. It means "to sharpen your appetite", as a whetstone sharpens a knife.

Reference: (http://www.phrases.org.uk/meanings/whet-your-appetite.html)

177.

There is a heavy-metal band called Okilly Dokilly that plays "Nedal" music, which is metal music themed around the character Ned Flanders. All five of the band's members perform dressed as Flanders, and the majority of their lyrics are Flanders quotes.

Reference: (https://en.wikipedia.org/wiki/Okilly_Dokilly)

178.

Gene Simmons is actually from Israel and is named Chaim Witz.

Reference: (https://en.wikipedia.org/wiki/Gene_Simmons)

179.

Coke was sued for the "unwarranted health claims" on their product Vitaminwater. Coke's defense was "no consumer could reasonably be misled into thinking Vitaminwater was a healthy beverage."

Reference: (http://www.huffingtonpost.com/john-robbins/the-dark-side-of-vitaminw_b_669716.html)

180.

There was an Olympic sport called "Plunge for Distance" that solely made an appearance in the 1904 summer games where "plungers" would compete by simply diving into a pool and float as far as they could with one breath.

Reference: (http://america.pink/plunge-for-distance_3538115.html)

181.

The first American spy satellites literally dropped their film from space in a "film bucket" that was then scooped up in midair by a plane.

Reference: (https://en.wikipedia.org/wiki/Corona_%28satellite%29)

182.

In 2012, the remains of King Richard III were found buried beneath a parking lot.

Reference: (https://en.wikipedia.org/wiki/Richard_III_of_England)

183.

Fritos Feet is a bacterial phenomenon that affects most dogs by making their feet smell like Fritos.

Reference: (http://dogwalkingdunfermline.org.uk/does-your-dog-have-frito-feet/)

184.

There's a Christian Mingle official movie.

Reference: (https://www.youtube.com/watch?v=E10Vo42MJEc)

185.

In 1965, two astronauts on their way back to orbit played a joke on mission control, pretending to spot Santa in space.

Reference:
(http://en.wikipedia.org/wiki/Gemini_6A#A_Christmas_surprise)

186.

Having a fetish for human hair is called trchophillia.

Reference: (https://en.wikipedia.org/wiki/Hair_fetishism)

187.

Ibiza tourism officials were "annoyed" by Mike Posner's "I Took a Pill in Ibiza", feeling it contributed to Ibiza's drug-related reputation.

Reference:
(https://en.wikipedia.org/wiki/I_Took_a_Pill_in_Ibiza#Controversy)

188.

21 cities and factories were targets for strategic nuclear bombing by the Germans in World War II via the "Amerika Bomber."

Reference: (https://en.wikipedia.org/wiki/Amerika_Bomber)

189.

In 1983, a man confessed to his wife's murder after part of a female skull was discovered in a peat bog near their home in England. He was convicted based on this confession. The skull turned out to be from someone who actually died 1750 years earlier.

Reference: (http://en.wikipedia.org/wiki/Lindow_Woman)

190.

In 1983, the British government deployed snipers to hunt and kill the Beast of Exmoor, an unidentified big cat believed to stalk the hills of South-West England.

Reference:
(https://en.wikipedia.org/wiki/Beast_of_Exmoor#Government_invol
vement)

191.

Carpatho-Ukraine is a state which was only independent for 24 hours. Its independence was declared on March 15th, 1939, but it was invaded by Hungary the next day.

Reference: (http://bigthink.com/strange-maps/57-carpatho-ukraine-independent-for-only-24-hours)

192.

In order to freeze-dry food, it must be heated.

Reference: (https://en.wikipedia.org/wiki/Freeze-drying)

193.

The best charities are often 10,000% more effective than average ones.

Reference: (http://www.forbes.com/sites/learnvest/2012/12/14/why-your-charitable-donations-probably-arent-doing-much-good/#204dca2f3bf2)

194.

There is a cat sanctuary at Tore Argentina, the ancient Roman square where Julius Caesar was assassinated.

Reference: (http://www.romancats.com/index_eng.php)

195.

Scientists gave a mouse cancer, then cured it with AIDS.

Reference: (http://io9.com/5308691/scientists-use-the-aids-virus-to-cure-cancer)

196.

There's a concept called "double depression," which describes when someone already suffering from clinical depression experiences an even worse major depressive episode.

Reference:
(https://en.wikipedia.org/wiki/Dysthymia#Double_depression)

197.

In World War I, soldiers were paired up to clean each other's feet in order to prevent trench foot.

Reference: (https://en.wikipedia.org/wiki/Trench_foot#Prevention)

198.

There is a much greater variety of sizes in condoms than just "regular" or "magnum," taking into account length and girth.

Reference: (http://learn.condomdepot.com/condom-size-chart/)

199.

A dog called Bobbie traveled over 2,500 miles across America to get back to his owners after being accidentally abandoned.

Reference:
(http://en.wikipedia.org/w/index.php?title=Bobbie_the_Wonder_Dog)

200.

The Goofy Stance comes from the 1937 Disney animation Hawaiian Holiday where Goofy's most successful attempt at surfing was with his right foot forward.

Reference:
(https://www.youtube.com/watch?v=SdIaEQCUVbk&feature=youtu.be)

201.

Robert Downey Jr. was arrested in 1999 for multiple drug charges. When in front of the judge, he said he had been addicted to drugs since the age of eight, due to the fact that his father, also an addict, had been giving them to him.

Reference:(https://en.wikipedia.org/wiki/Robert_Downey_Jr.#Begin
nings_and_critical_acclaim)

202.

Roy Orbison wore sunglasses when performing simply because he
had left his eyeglasses on an airplane. This forced him to wear his
prescription sunglasses on stage, and he found he preferred it.

Reference:
(https://en.wikipedia.org/wiki/Roy_Orbison#Developing_the_image)

203.

In 1943, Georgia became the first state to lower its voting age in
state and local elections from 21 to 18.

Reference: (https://en.wikipedia.org/wiki/Twenty-
sixth_Amendment_to_the_United_States_Constitution??)

204.

4 percent of Americans believe that shape-shifting "Lizard People"
are in political control of the US and the world. 7 percent were
unsure.

Reference: (http://www.vox.com/2014/11/5/7158371/lizard-people-
conspiracy-theory-explainer/)

205.

In 2005, a group of artists in Italy made a giant plush bunny and left
it on a hill in rural Italy. It's still there.

Reference: (http://time.com/94632/this-creepy-200-foot-stuffed-
rabbit-is-decaying-atop-an-italian-mountain)

206.

In 1939, over 750,000 pets across Britain were killed by their owners
after the government created the NARPAC, National Air Raid

Precautions Animal Committee, and released a pamphlet called "Advice to Animal Owners".

Reference: (https://en.wikipedia.org/wiki/British_Pet_Holocaust)

207.

The American Alligator's scientific name is "Alligator Mississippiensis".

Reference: (https://en.wikipedia.org/wiki/American_alligator)

208.

Frank's Hot Sauce is 120 years old.

Reference:
(https://en.wikipedia.org/wiki/Frank%27s_RedHot#History)

209.

An astronaut threw a boomerang while in a space station and it returned to him. As long as there is air to provide the necessary forces, a boomerang will return to its thrower, even in the weightlessness of Earth's orbit.

Reference: (http://www.newscientist.com/article/dn13525-does-a-boomerang-thrown-in-space-return-to-its-pitcher.html#.VLYQMSvF98G)

210.

The actress that played Katie O'Gill in the Disney classic "Darby O'Gill and the Little People" died young of Ischemic heart disease.

Reference: (https://en.wikipedia.org/wiki/Janet_Munro)

211.

Only 9% of suicide attempts are successful.

Reference: (https://www.hsph.harvard.edu/means-matter/means-matter/case-fatality/)

212.

TBS speeds up shows up to 9% to gain extra commercial ad time.

Reference:
(https://www.youtube.com/watch?v=z6i1VVikRu0&feature=youtu.be)

213.

The TU-95 Bomber flew its first combat mission nearly 60 years after it first entered service.

Reference: (https://en.wikipedia.org/wiki/Tupolev_Tu-95#Present_and_future_status)

214.

On October 21st, 2001, a Royal Canadian Navy ship, the HSMC Cape Breton, was sunk with explosives to create an artificial reef. Currently, it's a popular scuba site.

Reference: (https://www.youtube.com/watch?v=VETwT57d5I8)

215.

Heather Graham's parents forbid her from being in the movie "Heathers" because the script had too many expletives.

Reference: (https://en.wikipedia.org/wiki/Heather_Graham)

216.

The Hoia Baciu Forest is a forest in Romania where visitors have reported apparitions, UFOs, loss of time or memory, being physically scratched and seeing a circle in the middle of the forest where nothing ever grows. Some people have disappeared in the forest as well.

Reference: (https://hoiabaciuforest.com/)

217.

"Stylites" are early Christian ascetics in Syria and Asia Minor who climbed and lived on stone columns, where they preached to gathering crowds. Stylites may have influenced the later use of minarets in Islam.

Reference: (https://en.wikipedia.org/wiki/Stylite)

218.

The American Society of Composers, Authors and Publishers sued the Boy Scouts and Girl Scouts for singing copyrighted songs at camp without paying licensing fees. They also tried to sue people for copyright infringement on ringtones.

Reference:(https://en.wikipedia.org/wiki/American_Society_of_Com posers,_Authors_and_Publishers#Criticism)

219.

Lethal hypothermia victims can sometimes be misidentified as victims of violent crimes because of Paradoxical Undressing and Terminal Burrowing Behavior.

Reference:
(http://www.weirduniverse.net/blog/permalink/paradoxical_undressi ng/)

220.

Multiple sclerosis is an unpredictable disease that effects nearly 2.5 million people worldwide, with about 200 new cases every week in just the United States alone.

Reference: (http://main.nationalmssociety.org/goto/decker_austin)

221.

Most initial reports about Yellowstone were received as myths.

Reference:
(https://en.wikipedia.org/wiki/Yellowstone_National_Park#History)

222.

The origins of spiked dog collars came from "wolf collars", which were designed to protect dog's throats from a wolf attack.

Reference: (https://en.wikipedia.org/wiki/Wolf_collar)

223.

The KM Caspian Sea Monster was a Soviet era airplane that flew 20 feet above the Caspian Sea using ground effect. It had a max takeoff weight of 544 tons, and could reach speeds in excess of 300 MPH. It was intended for use by the military and rescue teams.

Reference: (https://www.youtube.com/watch?v=V8Nu94khHoo)

224.

In 1923, Jockey Frank Hayed had a heart attack and died in the middle of a race. His horse won the race while Hayes' body remained in the saddle, making him the first and only jockey to win a race after death. Apparently, he never won a race before that.

Reference: (http://mentalfloss.com/article/17647/eight-and-half-people-whose-jobs-actually-killed-them)

225.

Polar bear liver contains toxically high levels of vitamin A.

Reference: (http://animals.howstuffworks.com/mammals/eat-polar-bear-liver.htm)

226.

S. Korea, 41%, Japan, 28.9%, and China, 24%, account for more than 90% of the global shipbuilding industry.

Reference:
(https://en.wikipedia.org/wiki/Shipbuilding#Present_day_shipbuildin g)

227.

A number of studies found out that in order to stay drier in rain it's better to run than to walk; it also depends on an individual's height-to-breadth ratio as well as wind direction and raindrop size. If you're really thin, it's more probable that there will be an optimal running speed.

Reference: (http://www.bbc.com/news/science-environment-18901072)

228.

In 1520, in a meeting set to improve relations between France and England, Henry VIII challenged Francis I in a wrestling match, which he quickly lost.

Reference:
(https://en.wikipedia.org/wiki/Field_of_the_Cloth_of_Gold#Conseq uences)

229.

4 states (Vermont, Alaska, Hawaii, and Maine) have laws prohibiting the use of outdoor advertising with billboards.

Reference:
(http://en.wikipedia.org/wiki/Billboard#Laws_limiting_billboards)

230.

In 2011, Norway had a "butter crisis," with an acute shortage of butter which resulted in prices soaring.

Reference: (https://en.wikipedia.org/wiki/Norwegian_butter_crisis)

231.

Jimmy Carter's brother, Billy Carter, urinated in public in front of a group of reporters and dignitaries.

Reference: (http://mentalfloss.com/article/19202/6-presidential-siblings-and-headaches-they-caused)

232.

People on the south Pacific Pitcairn Islands, descended from British mutineers and accompanying Tahitians, speak an English creole that is heavily influenced by naval lingo. "To fall over" is "to capsize" while for "everyone" they say "all hands", from "all hands on deck".

Reference: (https://it.wikipedia.org/wiki/Pitcairn#Cultura)

233.

The majority of a whale's head is the "melon", which is an organ that amplifies echolocation.

Reference: (https://en.wikipedia.org/wiki/Melon_(cetacean))

234.

In 2007, a 75 year old woman from Virginia named Mona Shaw, smashed up a Comcast office with a hammer from being fed up with their poor customer service.

Reference: (http://www.nbcnews.com/id/21379720/ns/business-us_business/t/woman-fined-hammering-comcast-office/)

235.

A woman's history of vaginal orgasms is discernible from her walk.

Reference: (http://www.ncbi.nlm.nih.gov/m/pubmed/18637995/)

236.

There is a medieval forest preserved at the bottom of Fallen Leaf Lake due effects of a centuries-long Sierra Nevada mega drought.

Reference: (http://www.hcn.org/issues/44.22/underwater-forest-reveals-the-story-of-a-historic-megadrought)

237.

Female hyenas have a pseudo-penis.

Reference: (http://weirdanimalreport.com/article/female-hyenas-mock-penis)

238.

In 2011, Afghanistan's president, Hamid Karzai, pardoned dozens of child suicide bombers, and in February, 2012, many of the pardoned children were re-arrested attempting to commit suicide bombings in the Kandahar Province.

Reference:
(http://latimesblogs.latimes.com/world_now/2012/02/afghanistan-would-be-child-bombers-arrested-again.html)

239.

After a bone marrow transplant, the patient's blood type will change to the donor's blood type.

Reference:
(https://bethematch.org/apps/intheknow/donation.html#section7)

240.

IKEA's headquarters are in the Netherlands and not Sweden.

Reference: (https://en.wikipedia.org/wiki/IKEA)

241.

There's a form of Shark Fin Soup called "Buddha Jumps Over the Wall".

Reference:
(https://en.wikipedia.org/wiki/Buddha_Jumps_Over_the_Wall)

242.

Twi, the most spoken language in Ghana, is taught at Fordham University in New York.

Reference:
(http://legacy.fordham.edu/campus_resources/enewsroom/topstories_1731.asp)

243.

The Empire State Building was supposed to have a docking station for zeppelins at the spire of the building where passengers could enter and exit the airship through the observation platform. It was ultimately never built but the foundations for the dock are still there.

Reference:
(http://www.nytimes.com/2010/09/26/realestate/26scapes.html)

244.

A grotesque is not a gargoyle unless it is also a waterspout.

Reference:
(http://rmc.library.cornell.edu/adw/gravely/gargoyle.html)

245.

The closest election that had over 1 million voters was the Washington gubernatorial election in 2004. The difference was 133 votes out of 2.8 million.

Reference:
(https://en.wikipedia.org/wiki/Washington_gubernatorial_election,_
2004)

246.

When Princess Diana was stripped of the title "Her Royal Highness",
a young Prince William told his mother, "don't worry, mummy, I
will give it back to you one day when I am king."

Reference: (http://www.newsweek.com/what-princess-dianas-life-
might-look-now-67971)

247.

There are more dogs than children in San Francisco, according to the
U.S. Census Bureau.

Reference: (http://www.sfgate.com/news/article/S-F-S-BEST-
FRIEND-Where-pooches-outnumber-2555688.php?forceWeb=1)

248.

The Greek physician Galen wrote that, "Every animal is sad after
intercourse except the human female and the rooster".

Reference: (https://en.wikipedia.org/wiki/Post-coital_tristesse)

249.

In 1972, some of Aircraft Carrier USS Ranger's crew carried out
two-dozen acts of sabotage to prevent the ship from returning to
Vietnam.

Reference: (https://en.wikipedia.org/wiki/USS_Ranger_%28CV-
61%29#1970s)

250.

Arc Furnaces use electricity to heat and melt steel. These furnaces are more efficient for melting down scrap steel that blast furnaces, and can quickly be turned on and off.

Reference: (https://en.wikipedia.org/wiki/Electric_arc_furnace)

251.

Dr. Seuss wrote and illustrated a book for adults titled "The Seven Lady Godivas: The True Facts Concerning History's Barest Family".

Reference:
(http://www.theatlantic.com/entertainment/archive/2012/03/dr-seusss-little-known-book-of-nudes/253891/)

252.

After an 8 week course in mindfulness meditation, the amygdala, associated with fear and emotion, shrinks, while the pre-frontal cortex, associated with awareness, concentration and decision-making, becomes thicker.

Reference: (http://blogs.scientificamerican.com/guest-blog/2014/06/12/what-does-mindfulness-meditation-do-to-your-brain/)

253.

There used to be a medical device lined with radioactive materials used to irradiate water for drinking as it was believed to have great health benefits.

Reference: (https://en.wikipedia.org/wiki/Radium_Ore_Revigator)

254.

Ancient Rome at its peak was the most populous city in Europe until the 19th century.

Reference:
([https://en.wikipedia.org/wiki/List_of_largest_European_cities_in_hi story](https://en.wikipedia.org/wiki/List_of_largest_European_cities_in_history))

255.

The same Colorado hotel that inspired Stephen King to write, "The Shining", was used for filming Dumb and Dumber 20 years later.

Reference:
(https://en.wikipedia.org/wiki/The_Stanley_Hotel#The_Shining.2C_Stephen_King)

256.

"Musk" is the name given to a substance with a penetrating odor obtained from a gland of the male musk deer.

Reference: (https://en.wikipedia.org/wiki/Musk)

257.

70% of the land in the U.K. is owned by less than 1% of the people, who are mostly descended from Normans.

Reference:
(http://www.theguardian.com/commentisfree/2012/dec/17/high-house-prices-inequality-normans)

258.

A helicopter's classic beating sound is actually a series of mini sonic booms created by the tips of the rotor blades travelling at supersonic speeds.

Reference:
(https://www.youtube.com/watch?v=LDrk9Ssz9_E&feature=youtu.be&t=948)

259.

More Africans have access to cell phone service than piped water. 63% have access to piped water. Yet, 93% of Africans have cell phone service.

Reference: (http://www.cnn.com/2016/01/19/africa/africa-afrobarometer-infrastructure-report/)

260.

From 1954 to 1975, Hoover sold a small spherical vacuum cleaner that acted as a hovercraft; it lacked wheels and floated on its downward-facing exhaust. They worked well on both carpeted and hardwood floors. A modern version was sold in the U.S. and U.K. from 2006 to 2009.

Reference:
(https://en.wikipedia.org/wiki/Vacuum_cleaner#Constellation)

261.

Studies show that an increase in Facebook usage is heavily linked to decrease in satisfaction with your own life and higher likelihood of depression.

Reference: (http://guardianlv.com/2013/08/facebook-causes-depression-new-study-says/)

262.

Starboard is named after the old English words for "steer" and "side of the boat" because most sailors were right handed, so the steering oar was on the right side.

Reference: (http://oceanservice.noaa.gov/facts/port-starboard.html)

263.

Dwarf elephants, around 3.5 feet tall, existed on many of the Mediterranean islands during the Pleistocene period, 2,588,000 to 11,700 years ago.

Reference: (https://en.wikipedia.org/wiki/Dwarf_elephant)

264.

Crows are monogamous and raise families together. Offspring from previous seasons even remain with the family to help rear new nestlings.

Reference:
(http://en.wikipedia.org/wiki/American_crow#Reproduction)

265.

Although it is against tradition, an Australian Prime Minister can be a member of the upper house, and this has already occurred for a short time following the disappearance of Harold Holt.

Reference: (https://en.wikipedia.org/wiki/John_Gorton)

266.

There exists a subsolar point, a set of points across Earth's surface, spread throughout the plane depending upon the time of a day, on which Sun shadow is invisible, or where the sun's rays are hitting the planet exactly perpendicular to its surface.

Reference: (https://en.wikipedia.org/wiki/Subsolar_point)

267.

The Kodak Company used a 13 month calendar from 1924 to 1989 and George Eastman pushed for its worldwide acceptance.

Reference: (http://www.citylab.com/work/2014/12/the-world-almost-had-a-13-month-calendar/383610/)

268.

The energy output from 1 gram of uranium used in nuclear power plants is equivalent to that from 3 tons of coal, or 300 gallons of oil.

Reference: (http://www2.lbl.gov/abc/wallchart/chapters/14/1.html)

269.

Jonathon Levin was a High School English teacher in the Bronx who was murdered by one of his own students after mentioning to his class that he was the son of TWC CEO, Gerald Levin. He was murdered because his killer assumed he was wealthy, but he only managed to steal $800.

Reference: (https://en.wikipedia.org/wiki/Gerald_M._Levin)

270.

We call meat between two pieces of bread a "sandwich", because the Earl of Sandwich wanted to try that combination and other people copied it.

Reference:
(https://www.wyzant.com/resources/lessons/english/etymology/words-mod-sandwich)

271.

In 1965, 47 year old lawyer Andre-Francois Raffray agreed to pay Jeanne Calment a rent of $500 a month until she died, on the condition that he would inherit her house afterwards. Raffray died in 1995, at age 77 while Calment was still alive at age 120.

Reference: (http://articles.chicagotribune.com/1995-12-27/news/9512280029_1_jeanne-calment-elderly-woman-christmas-day)

272.

The 1993 bombings in Warrington, England, that killed two children is thought to have been carried out by the IRA and a British Leftist political group, Red Action.

Reference: (https://en.wikipedia.org/wiki/Red_Action)

273.

A high school in Utah allowed students to use a real gun, loaded with blank rounds, in a high school production of Oklahoma. A student ended up shooting himself in the head with it, not knowing that a blank gun can still kill at close range.

Reference:(http://blogs.edweek.org/edweek/school_law/2012/05/court_allows_suit_over_school_.html?qs=)

274.

Augustus Caesar, who founded the Roman Empire, also created the first institutionalized police force and firefighting force.

Reference: (https://en.wikipedia.org/wiki/Augustus)

275.

If a snake gets too hot then it may get so confused that it mistakes its tail for prey, and tries to eat itself until it dies.

Reference: (http://www.iflscience.com/plants-and-animals/stressed-out-snake-eats-itself/)

276.

Freddie Mercury once dressed Princess Diana up as a man and took her out clubbing. Nobody recognized her.

Reference:(http://books.google.com/books?id=jvz_iqblAYC&lpg=PA1&pg=PT42&redir_esc=y#v=onepage&q&f=false)

277.

The color you see in total darkness is not black, but a dark gray called "eigengrau".

Reference: (https://en.wikipedia.org/wiki/Eigengrau)

278.

Brian May built his first guitar from a bit of Fireplace, Table Top, Knitting Needle and other scraps.

Reference: (https://www.youtube.com/watch?v=cPD7_hQk7hk)

279.

There has been a number of long term studies on the possibility of dosing food in radiation as a form of preservation and sterilization. However, while it has been found to be completely safe, there is a large resistance to it because of the negative impression of and confusion over radiation.

Reference: (http://en.wikipedia.org/wiki/Food_irradiation)

280.

The Art Deco spire on top of the Empire State Building was originally designed to be a mooring mast, disembarkation terminal, and a depot for dirigibles.

Reference:(https://en.wikipedia.org/wiki/Empire_State_Building#Di rigible_.28airship.29_terminal)

281.

The Irish cargo ship MV Kerlogue, designed for short coastal journeys, was forced to undertake far longer ones due to Ireland's lack of ships during World War II. On separate occasions, it was attacked by both Allied and Axis forces and also rescued both Allied and Axis personnel.

Reference: (https://en.wikipedia.org/wiki/MV_Kerlogue)

282.

167 people cashed in big on 175 to 1 odds that Luis Suarez would bite someone during the 2014 World Cup after a Norwegian betting side posted a joke bet.

Reference: (http://ftw.usatoday.com/2014/06/luis-suarez-biting-prop-bet-norway)

283.

Jason Alexander, who played George Costanza in Seinfeld, had a lifelong desire to be in a Disney film and had a supporting role in "The Hunchback of Notre Dame." He reprised his role in Kingdom Hearts.

Reference:(https://en.wikipedia.org/wiki/The_Hunchback_of_Notre_Dame_(1996_film)#Casting)

284.

WALL-E is in loving memory of one of the animators, Justin Wright.

Reference: (https://en.wikipedia.org/wiki/Justin_Wright)

285.

An ex-member of Pink Floyd, in "a real act of mad genius," pranked the band by writing a seemingly simple song that the band could never learn; each time they rehearsed it, he would arbitrarily change the chords, then sing it back to them to correct them. It was called "Have You Got It Yet?"

Reference:
(https://en.wikipedia.org/wiki/Syd_Barrett#Departure_from_Pink_Floyd)

286.

Women can accurately guess the symmetry of a man's face by the smell of their t-shirt.

Reference:
(http://www.psychologicalscience.org/pdf/onlyhuman/sleeping_ene
my.pdf)

287.

The city of Los Angeles spends an estimated $100 million dollars per year on homelessness.

Reference:(https://en.wikipedia.org/wiki/Homelessness_in_the_Unit
ed_States#Los_Angeles.2C_California)

288.

A popular slang word in French for having your period is "Les Anglais ont debarqué", or, "The English have landed".

Reference: (http://french.about.com/od/intvocab/fl/Menstrual-Time-
To-Have-Your-Period-in-French-And-Hygienic-Vocabulary.htm)

289.

Albert Hofmann, the founder of LSD, was also the first person to identify and isolate psilocybin, the active ingredient in magic mushrooms.

Reference:
(http://www.neuroscientificallychallenged.com/blog/2014/5/12/magi
c-mushrooms-and-the-amygdala)

290.

Besides solid, liquid, gas and plasma, there are other states of matter, called "degenerate matter".

Reference: (https://en.wikipedia.org/wiki/Degenerate_matter)

291.

Rainey Bethea, who was hanged August 14th, 1938, was the first person to be publicly executed by a woman, and also the last person to be publicly executed in the United States.

Reference: (https://en.wikipedia.org/wiki/Rainey_Bethea)

292.

A Californian couple sailed to one of the most remote islands in the world, expecting to find themselves alone for a year. Instead, a fugitive stole their boat and murdered them.

Reference: (http://en.wikipedia.org/wiki/And_the_Sea_Will_Tell)

293.

The plural noun version of "stadium" is "stadia".

Reference: (https://en.wikipedia.org/wiki/Stadia)

294.

The members of the original Lord of the Rings: Fellowship of the Ring all received tattoos reading "nine" in Elvish upon the series' completion, except the actor who played Gimly.

Reference: (https://www.tattoodo.com/a/2015/07/the-matching-tattoos-of-the-lord-of-the-rings-cast/)

295.

Humans have an instinctual biochemical reaction to baby features in animals – big eyes, proportionately big heads, etc. – that produces maternalistic emotions. Disney has exploited this instinct in every movie.

Reference:
(https://www.animalsciencepublications.org/publications/af/articles/4/3/32)

296.

"Dilbert" cartoonist Scott Adams once published a self-promoting op-ed in the Wall Street Journal, for which he was mocked by his own fans on his web forum. One user defended Adams, accusing the others of being jealous of Adams' "genius." The user was outed as Adams himself, using a pseudonym.

Reference: (http://jezebel.com/5792583/dilbert-creator-pretends-to-be-his-own-biggest-fan-on-message-boards)

297.

The Governator was almost a TV Series by Stan Lee featuring "cyber security expert, Zeke Muckerberg".

Reference: (https://en.wikipedia.org/wiki/The_Governator#History#)

298.

1816 was the "Year Without Summer". Snow fell all summer from New England to as far south as Virginia. This may have been due to the Tambora volcano, which erupted for a week.

Reference:
(http://history1800s.about.com/od/crimesanddisasters/a/The-Year-Without-A-Summer.htm)

299.

Camp X, the training camp for the American OSS, Office of Strategic Services, forerunner to the CIA, during World War II, opened on December 6th, 1941. One day later, the Japanese attacked Pearl Harbor.

Reference: (https://en.wikipedia.org/wiki/Camp_X)

300.

Pennsylvania had a soccer team called the Pennsylvania Stoners.

Reference: (https://en.wikipedia.org/wiki/Pennsylvania_Stoners)

301.

John F. Kennedy's sister, Rosemary Kennedy, was given a lobotomy because their father, Joseph P. Kennedy, was especially worried that his daughter's behavior would bring shame and embarrassment upon the family and possibly damage his political career.

Reference: (https://en.wikipedia.org/wiki/Rosemary_Kennedy)

302.

Axl Rose's mother was 16 years old and still in high school when she had him, the father was 20 years old. Pregnancy was unplanned and his parents separated when Rose was 2 years old, prompting his father to abduct and allegedly molest him before disappearing.

Reference:(https://en.wikipedia.org/w/index.php?title=Axl_Rose&mobileaction=toggle_view_desktop#Early_life)

303.

The speed of sound is about 4 times faster in water.

Reference: (https://en.wikipedia.org/wiki/Speed_of_sound)

304.

General Motors had a version of OnStar in the 1960s.

Reference: (http://wheels.blogs.nytimes.com/2013/08/05/g-m-had-a-version-of-onstar-in-1966/)

305.

The unicorn is Scotland's national animal.

Reference: (http://www.scotsman.com/heritage/people-places/scottish-fact-of-the-week-scotland-s-official-animal-the-unicorn-1-2564399)

306.

The longest extra time that was given in football is 23 minutes, due to a broken leg, a dislocated shoulder and serious concussion.

Reference:
(https://www.theguardian.com/football/2006/nov/29/theknowledge.sport)

307.

Designers wanted their models to look like they were on heroin in the mid-90s. The look, characterized by pale skin, dark circles underneath the eyes and angular bone structure, was a reaction against the "healthy" and vibrant look of models such as Cindy Crawford and Claudia Schiffer.

Reference: (http://en.wikipedia.org/wiki/Heroin_chic)

308.

We use over 368 trillion gallons of water annually to process coal.

Reference: (https://en.wikipedia.org/wiki/Coal_slurry)

309.

The term Ostalgie refers to nostalgia for aspects of life in Socialist East Germany. It is a portmanteau of the German words Nostalgie, meaning nostalgia, and Ost, meaning east.

Reference: (https://en.wikipedia.org/wiki/Ostalgie)

310.

9000 people follow a twitter account called "Cologne Cathedral" that tweets "DONG" every hour. The amount of "DONGs" shows the time.

Reference: (https://twitter.com/koelner_dom)

311.

Hotel Heiress and Reality TV personality Paris Hilton released an album that hit number 6 on Billboard 200, selling more than 600,000 copies worldwide.

Reference:
(https://en.wikipedia.org/wiki/Paris_(Paris_Hilton_album))

312.

Alnwick Garden, in Northern England, is considered the most deadly garden on Earth and is a tourist attraction. Over 100 toxic plants are on walk through display, including species that can cause guests to fall unconsciousness from toxic fumes.

Reference: (http://www.smithsonianmag.com/travel/step-inside-worlds-most-dangerous-garden-if-you-dare-180952635/?no-ist)

313.

In 2010, George Lucas said, "I am dedicating the majority of my wealth to improving education. It is the key to the survival of the human race." Two years later, Lucas sold Lucasfilm Ltd. to Disney for $4.05 billion dollars and donated the proceeds to a charity that focuses on education.

Reference:
(http://www.forbes.com/sites/briansolomon/2012/11/04/donating-star-wars-billions-will-make-george-lucas-one-of-the-biggest-givers-ever/)

314.

Edmund Hillary and Tenzing Norgay were very nearly not the first to set foot on the top of Mount Everest; two other members of their expedition who were ahead of them made it to within 91 vertical meters of the summit before having to turn back.

Reference:
(https://en.wikipedia.org/wiki/Tenzing_Norgay#Success_on_Mount_Everest)

315.

John Christian killed his junior high teacher in 1978 when he was 13. The killer was diagnosed with mental illness and is currently residing as a lawyer in Austin, Texas.

Reference: (http://www.michaelcorcoran.net/archives/1469)

316.

Teddy Roosevelt once held the world record for the most handshakes in a single day, with 8,510 handshakes at a White House reception.

Reference: (https://en.wikipedia.org/wiki/Handshake#Records)

317.

The "Goldwater Rule" prevents mental health professionals from giving a diagnosis of public figures that they have not treated themselves.

Reference:
(http://psychnews.psychiatryonline.org/doi/full/10.1176%2Fpn.42.10.0002)

318.

The band Blood on the Dance Floor is from Orlando, Florida.

Reference:
(https://en.wikipedia.org/wiki/Blood_on_the_Dance_Floor_(duo))

319.

Saudi Arabia has topped the list of global nations that are supporting humanitarian works and it has recently donated 0.5% of its national income for that very purpose.

Reference: (http://www.arabnews.com/saudi-arabia/news/793896)

320.

The highest-flying Space Shuttle was Discovery in 1990, when it deployed the Hubble Space Telescope at 612 kilometers above the Earth. For comparison, the ISS orbits at an average altitude of 400 kilometers.

Reference: (https://en.wikipedia.org/wiki/STS-31#Mission_highlights)

321.

When Janet Leigh saw herself on the screen in Alfred Hitchcock's classic horror film "Psycho," she was so traumatized that she never took another shower.

Reference: (http://www.nytimes.com/1995/05/01/movies/psycho-in-janet-leigh-s-psyche.html)

322.

There's an island in the pacific where many of the residents are completely color blind, only being able to perceive black and white colors. However, they often take a psychedelic drug which allows them to perceive colored hallucinations.

Reference: (http://www.color-blindness.com/2011/11/14/living-with-total-color-blindness-documentary-island-of-the-colorblind/)

323.

The Wachowskis Brothers, directors of the Matrix, have both transitioned to female.

Reference: (http://www.hollywoodreporter.com/news/second-wachowski-sibling-comes-as-873674)

324.

Bitch Wars was a gulag based, Russian Mafia led war between prisoners that refused to fight for Stalin during World War II, and the prisoners that agreed to fight for their freedom.

Reference: (https://en.wikipedia.org/wiki/Bitch_Wars)

325.

Because of Valentine's Day, March is the biggest month for pregnancy test sales.

Reference: (http://www.bbdirect.com/blog/valentines-day-data-people-love-and-money)

326.

Having bird nests on or near your home can lead to an infestation of bird mites throughout the whole house, and parasitic infestation of the human host.

Reference: (http://www.birdmites.org/)

327.

Noni G. Bose, father of Amar Bose, founder of the Bose Corporation, was very active during the Indian Revolutionary Movement against the Colonial British and fled to the U.S. in 1920s to avoid persecution by the British.

Reference: (https://en.wikipedia.org/wiki/Amar_Bose)

328.

Mobile users in poor countries can access Wikipedia articles without data charges thanks to "Wikipedia Zero". It is currently operating in 34 countries.

Reference: (http://wikimediafoundation.org/wiki/Wikipedia_Zero)

329.

Lichen, a greenish composite organism of fungus and algae usually found on trees indicates good air quality.

Reference: (http://www.air-quality.org.uk/19.php)

330.

William Chaloner was a 17th century British con artist whom Isaac Newton proved guilty of high treason.

Reference: (https://en.wikipedia.org/wiki/William_Chaloner)

331.

David Prowse, the actor behind Darth Vader, was also the Green Cross Code Man.

Reference: (https://en.wikipedia.org/wiki/David_Prowse)

332.

A large number of critically injured victims of the 2012 Aurora Theater shooting were transported to hospitals in police cars instead of ambulances, likely saving their lives.

Reference:
(https://www.youtube.com/watch?v=R2zuvOfVc8Y&t=11m18s)

333.

Half the U.S. population are affected by piles, usually before the age of 50.

Reference: (http://www.medicalnewstoday.com/articles/239454.php)

334.

A study by UC Berkeley showed that experiencing art, spirituality, and nature are actually linked to lower levels of pro-inflammatory cytokine, which may prevent disease and other illnesses.

Reference: (http://artreport.com/the-power-of-art-and-how-it-may-prevent-disease/)

335.

The Football Association banned women's football in 1921 because it was more popular than men's.

Reference: (http://www.bbc.co.uk/news/magazine-30329606)

336.

A team from Norway and other Scandinavian countries made a Viking ship from scratch using Viking technology and sailed to North America to prove that the Vikings could do it, and they did.

Reference: (http://www.drakenexpeditionamerica.com/)

337.

Bruce Lee left Hong Kong for Seattle in 1958 with nothing but $100 in his pocket. He gave cha-cha lessons to first class passengers to earn extra money during the ship ride to the U.S.

Reference:
(http://www.imdb.com/name/nm0000045/bio?mode=desktop)

338.

India consumes 63% of the world's cumin.

Reference: (https://en.wikipedia.org/wiki/Cumin#Cultivation_areas)

339.

"Daggering" is an actual form of dance that involves dry humping, wrestling, and a decent amount of athleticism.

Reference: (https://www.youtube.com/watch?v=crhP0rgjdFU)

340.

Police in West Germany located a man who had a warrant for unpaid fines. They confronted him just as his slot machine struck a jackpot, and he avoided jail time by paying his fine on the spot.

Reference: (http://www.thelocal.de/20140926/slot-machine-saves-gambler-from-prison)

341.

Eating poppy seeds can cause a false positive in a urine test for opioids.

Reference:(http://www.ncbi.nlm.nih.gov/pubmed?term=morphine%20and%20codeine%20on%20poppy%20seeds%20thevis)

342.

Barbie dolls were originally a German gold-digging cartoon character.

Reference: (http://www.messynessychic.com/2016/01/29/meet-lilli-the-high-end-german-call-girl-who-became-americas-iconic-barbie-doll/)

343.

Hunter Gatherers experienced far more leisure time and far fewer hours of work than members of modern industrial society.

Reference: (http://en.wikipedia.org/wiki/Hunter-gatherer#Common_characteristics)

344.

People have been found dead casually sitting next to open electrical equipment; which means that they got a fatal shock to the heart but sat down because they only felt a little lightheaded.

Reference: (https://youtu.be/wR6g38Pxwog)

345.

With only 40 digits of Pi, you could calculate the circumference of the entire universe to within a single hydrogen atom.

Reference: (http://www.jpl.nasa.gov/edu/news/2016/3/16/how-many-decimals-of-pi-do-we-really-need/)

346.

The U.S. Department of Transportation considers the value of a statistical life at $9.1 million dollars.

Reference:(https://www.transportation.gov/sites/dot.dev/files/docs/VSL%20Guidance%202013.pdf)

347.

The island of Grenada was once invaded by the United States after a communist government took power.

Reference: (https://en.wikipedia.org/wiki/Invasion_of_Grenada)

348.

The spaghetti sandwich has been described as a "Tokyo novelty" and "handy commuter snack".

Reference: (https://en.wikipedia.org/wiki/Spaghetti_sandwich)

349.

In the Soviet Union, there was a video game console called the EKSI video 01 that had similar capabilities as Pong.

Reference:
(http://www.leningrad.su/museum/show_calc.php?n=402)

350.

Robert de Brus, 5th Lord of Annandale, was an unsuccessful competitor for the Scottish Crown in 1290. However, his grandson Robert the Bruce eventually became King of Scots.

Reference:
(https://en.wikipedia.org/wiki/Robert_de_Brus,_5th_Lord_of_Annan dale)

351.

When Amy Sedaris was 16 years old, she was fired for being 5 minutes late to her job. In order to take revenge on her boss, she threw his keys in the snow, and he only found them later in spring.

Reference: (https://en.wikipedia.org/wiki/Amy_Sedaris#Early_life)

352.

Vincent van Gogh painted "Starry Night" while he was in an insane asylum.

Reference: (http://discovermagazine.com/2006/oct/van-gogh-turbulence-painting)

353.

The first vote for the Baseball Hall of Fame had no unanimous inductees. The five inductees included Babe Ruth, Honus Wagner, and Ty Cobb.

Reference:
(https://en.wikipedia.org/wiki/Baseball_Hall_of_Fame_balloting,_19 36)

354.

A NASA employee, George Aldrich, has a job where he has to sniff things to check if they have an unpleasant smell before they can be flown to space.

Reference:([https://www.nasa.gov/centers/wstf/news/2011/GA_Wow](https://www.nasa.gov/centers/wstf/news/2011/GA_Wows_WSTF.html#.V2G1bDOxUwg) s_WSTF.html#.V2G1bDOxUwg)

355.

If we assume that only 5% of all the humans that will ever be born have already been born (about 60 billion), then we can predict that 1.2 trillion humans will ever be born. Assuming that the world population stabilizes at 10 billion at a life expectancy of 80 years, it can be estimated that the remaining 1.14 trillion humans that will ever be born will be born in 9120 years. This is the Doomsday Argument.

Reference: (http://en.wikipedia.org/wiki/Doomsday_argument)

356.

The Aztecs believed that dead warriors were reincarnated as hummingbirds, which is why their sun and war god, Huitzilopochtli, is represented as a hummingbird.

Reference: (http://www.britannica.com/topic/Huitzilopochtli)

357.

The asteroid that led to extinction of the dinosaurs hit the surface of the Earth near today's city of Chicxulub, Mexico.

Reference:([https://en.wikipedia.org/wiki/Cretaceous%E2%80%93Pa](https://en.wikipedia.org/wiki/Cretaceous%E2%80%93Paleogene_extinction_event#Chicxulub_asteroid_impact) leogene_extinction_event#Chicxulub_asteroid_impact)

358.

"Roasted Nuts" was the paper headline for when a mental hospital caught on fire.

Reference: (http://articles.philly.com/2002-07-12/news/25358011_1_breast-feeding-carwash-headline)

359.

Prior to the Battle of Antietam, two Union soldiers discovered Confederate battle plans along with cigars in an envelope.

Reference:
(https://en.wikipedia.org/wiki/Special_Order_191#History)

360.

An apartment building in China tipped over, but remained completely intact, after an excavation on the side of the building to create an underground parking garage weakened the foundation the building was built on and the rain washed the rest of the foundation away.

Reference:
(http://www.engineering.com/Library/ArticlesPage/tabid/85/ArticleID/410/Ever-see-a-12-story-building-just-fall-over.aspx)

361.

Belgium has 4 commonly spoken languages: Dutch, French, German and English. 38% of Belgians use 2 or 3 languages at work and 27% of Belgians can converse in more than 3 languages.

Reference: (http://www.amcham.be/blog/2013/09/multilingualism-belgium-competitive-advantage)

362.

The United States took possession of Wake Island by simply walking on it and raising the flag.

Reference:
(https://en.wikipedia.org/wiki/Wake_Island#American_possession)

363.

The prettiest side of your face is your left one. If you are going to take a side selfie, look at the camera from your left side.

Reference: (http://earthsky.org/human-world/which-side-of-your-face-is-better-looking-the-left-research-says)

364.

A trust fund for $1.5 million dollars was opened for high school students in the Canadian town of Lewisporte after they volunteered to help passengers of Delta Flight 15, which was flying back to the United States from Frankfurt when the September 11th attacks happened and the passengers were stuck in the town for 2 days.

Reference: (http://mytnnews.com/blog/2012/10/11/delta-flight-15-a-true-story-about-9-11/)

365.

Some cities in France have vending machines that dispense short stories instead of candy.

Reference: (http://nuvomagazine.com/culture/frances-short-story-dispensers)

366.

There is an "Apple Tree Colony" in Ukraine across 10,000 square feet consisting of only one tree that spread naturally by creating roots from its branches. Scientist have not been able to reproduce this with other apple trees.

Reference: (http://www.dogonews.com/2015/9/25/ukraines-unique-apple-tree-colony-comprises-one-ancient-apple-tree)

367.

When Steve Jobs refused to give early Apple employees stock, Steve Wozniak offered them $10 million worth of his.

Reference: (http://www.businessinsider.com/steve-wozniak-gave-early-apple-employees-10-million-in-stock-2014-9)

368.

Professors Yutaka Tahara and Katsuya Obara have developed a novel shell-less culture system for chick embryos using a plastic film as culture vessels.

Reference:
(https://www.jstage.jst.go.jp/article/jpsa/51/3/51_0130043/_article)

369.

Guy Fieri has a $200,000 booking fee.

Reference: (https://www.allamericanspeakers.com/speakers/Guy-Fieri/5469)

370.

The average person will walk approximately the distance of 3 times around the planet in their lifetime.

Reference: (http://en.wikipedia.org/w/index.php?title=Earth)

371.

80% of the Honda Accord and Toyota Camry is built in the United States; that's 20% more than the Ford F series trucks.

Reference: (http://builthere.us/how-american-is-my-car/)

372.

Kendrick Lamar's m.A.A.d city is an acronym for "me an Angel on Angel dust".

Reference: (https://en.wikipedia.org/wiki/M.A.A.D_City)

<h1 style="text-align:center">373.</h1>

A German art student illuminated and bound the entire Silmarillion by hand like a 21st century monastic scribe as his final project.

Reference: (http://makezine.com/2011/08/25/art-student-hand-illuminates-binds-a-copy-of-tolkiens-silmarillion/)

<h1 style="text-align:center">374.</h1>

The "Batman" was an Ottoman Unit of Measure. One Batman was equivalent to about 7.5 pounds.

Reference:
(https://en.wikipedia.org/wiki/Batman_(unit)#Ottoman_Empire)

<h1 style="text-align:center">375.</h1>

Disney published illustrated propaganda for nuclear energy, called Our Friend the Atom.

Reference: (https://www.brainpickings.org/2013/02/18/our-friend-the-atom-disney/)

<h1 style="text-align:center">376.</h1>

Tumbleweeds spread radiation from old nuclear sites.

Reference: (http://gizmodo.com/how-tumbleweeds-spread-radiation-from-old-nuclear-sites-1508617887)

<h1 style="text-align:center">377.</h1>

In 2012, a time capsule was discovered beneath the statue of Lenin in Kamchatka, Russia, some 33 years to the day after its burial. The message contained words of encouragement and confidence that the message's readers would be "better" than its writers, and would still be Communist.

Reference: (http://www.themoscowtimes.com/news/article/time-capsule-found-under-lenin-statue/462327.html)

378.

The CIA provided Indonesian death squads with lists of known communists' names during the Indonesian Genocide, a period that resulted in some 500,000 to one million deaths.

Reference:(https://en.wikipedia.org/wiki/Indonesian_killings_of_196 5%E2%80%9366#Foreign_involvement)

379.

Butterflies attach their eggs to leaves with an almost unbreakable glue, the chemical compounds of which we still don't understand.

Reference:
(http://www.todayifoundout.com/index.php/2011/10/caterpillars-melt-almost-completely-before-growing-into-butterflies-in-the-chrysalis/)

380.

Julia Stewart, who worked as a waitress at an IHOP at 16 years old, worked her way up through various jobs to become a President at Applebee's. After being passed over for CEO, she returned to IHOP, became CEO, and later acquired Applebee's.

Reference:
(http://abcnews.go.com/Business/CEOProfiles/story?id=4573076&page=1)

381.

A shandy is when you pour the lemonade first then add the beer. But, when the beer is poured first and then the lemonade is added, it's referred to a lemon topper.

Reference: (https://en.wikipedia.org/wiki/Shandy)

382.

When New York City Hall was renovated in 1903, a secret stairwell was discovered. It was said to be used by aldermen to escape the building when angry constituents were waiting for them outside.

Reference: (http://cdnc.ucr.edu/cgi-bin/cdnc?a=d&d=LAH19030731.2.20)

383.

In the 1870s, something very strange happened to the French-Canadians working as lumberjacks in Northern Maine. When startled, they would jump in the air.

Reference:
(https://en.wikipedia.org/wiki/Jumping_Frenchmen_of_Maine)

384.

Actor J.K Simmons has won 39 awards for his role in the movie Whiplash.

Reference:
(https://en.wikipedia.org/wiki/J._K._Simmons#Awards_and_nominations)

385.

In seasons 9 and 10 of the popular American sitcom 'Friends', each of the star cast members were paid $1 million per episode.

Reference: (http://en.wikipedia.org/w/index.php?title=Friends)

386.

In 2012, in Valencia, three Ryanair airplanes had to do an emergency landing due to low fuel amounts, because the company pressures the pilots to use the absolute minimum legal amount of fuel.

Reference:
(https://www.youtube.com/watch?v=EZEpVnWaI5E&feature=youtu
.be)

387.

In the 1990's, reusing medical equipment was a serious problem, particularly in China where as many as 250,000 blood and plasma donors were potentially exposed to HIV from shared needles.

Reference:
(https://en.wikipedia.org/wiki/Blood_donation#Complications)

388.

Researchers who measured the slipperiness of banana peels, the ability of pork strips to stop nosebleeds, and the reactions of reindeer to humans in polar bear suits were among the winners of 2014 Ig Nobel prizes.

Reference: (http://www.reuters.com/article/2014/09/19/us-usa-science-ignobelprizes-idUSKBN0HD2RT20140919)

389.

The world's biggest bonfire is built every year for the Midsummer's Feast in Ålesund, Norway. This year they're aiming for a bonfire 45 meters high.

Reference: (http://gianthum.com/pallets-bonfire-norway-john-baptist-midsummer/)

390.

The Angel of Nanjing was a selfless man who has patrolled the Yangtze River Bridge since 2003, saving people who wish to commit suicide and counselling them back to health, he has saved over 300 lives to this day.

Reference: (https://www.youtube.com/watch?v=kHxR4Q1Fp-c)

391.

Mathematically speaking, an infinite series of events can occur in a finite amount of time.

Reference: (http://plato.stanford.edu/entries/spacetime-supertasks/)

392.

Fingernails are much more permeable than skin.

Reference:
(https://en.wikipedia.org/wiki/Nail_(anatomy)#Permeability)

393.

A man's last words before swimming in alligator infested waters were, "[fuck] the alligators".

Reference:
(https://en.wikipedia.org/wiki/List_of_fatal_alligator_attacks_in_the_United_States)

394.

Contrary to popular belief, the Nazi's did welcome black North Africans and Middle-Eastern men to fight in their ranks within the Free Arabian Legion.

Reference: (https://en.wikipedia.org/wiki/Free_Arabian_Legion)

395.

An English horn isn't a horn but an oboe, and it's not even English, but French.

Reference: (https://en.wikipedia.org/wiki/Cor_anglais)

396.

The first anesthetic use of chloroform was by James Simpson, an obstetrician, who used chloroform on a pair of humans, who were guests at one of his dinner parties. This was not done as a medical procedure, but for entertainment.

Reference: (https://en.wikipedia.org/wiki/Chloroform#Anesthetic)

397.

Doctors induced labor to make sure that Kim Jong-Un's child was born in 2012, which marked the 100th anniversary of North Korean founder Kim Il-Sung.

Reference:
(http://english.chosun.com/site/data/html_dir/2013/03/20/2013032000553.html)

398.

The average density of the Sun is about the same as water.

Reference: (http://solar-center.stanford.edu/vitalstats.html)

399.

The Subway franchise was sued for a Hepatitis outbreak.

Reference: (http://www.about-hepatitis.com/hepatitis_outbreaks/news/lawsuit-filed-against-subway-in-hepatitis-outbreak/#.Vu3M8_krKUk)

400.

In November 2008, the discovery of an eye-witness account on how Hitler was treated after being shot on the Western Front during World War I was announced in the press. According to the report, Hitler was monorchid.

Reference:
(http://en.wikipedia.org/wiki/Adolf_Hitler%27s_possible_monorchis
m)

401.

The first apple pie recipe was found in an English cookbook in 1381, and the first recorded apple pie consumption in America occurred in 1697, meaning that well known phrase "American as Apple Pie" is a complete misconception.

Reference: (http://priceonomics.com/how-apple-pie-became-american/)

402.

More people speak Polish in Ireland than Irish.

Reference: (http://www.rte.ie/news/2012/0329/315449-divorce-rate-up-150-since-2002-census/)

403.

Australia's first police force was made up of the most well - behaved convicts.

Reference: (http://www.police.nsw.gov.au/about_us/history)

404.

There is a species of fish that can travel outside of water and breathe air.

Reference: (https://en.wikipedia.org/wiki/Walking_catfish)

405.

You can buy an American flag that has been flown over the Capitol.

Reference: (http://www.usflag.org/capitol.flag.html)

406.

Albert Einstein's eyeballs are in a safety deposit box in New York City. They are "owned" by his eye doctor, Henry Adams.

Reference: (http://jppreston.com/2011/12/14/einsteins-eyes-yeah-theyre-still-around/)

407.

There is a substance called Resiniferatoxin that is 16,000,000,000 scoville units. It is able to burn skin in microscopic amounts.

Reference: (http://pepperheadsforlife.com/resiniferatoxin/)

408.

Baseball has a rule which says players can't fraternize with the other team while in uniform.

Reference:
(http://www.wsj.com/articles/SB10001424052970203476804576614843432290036)

409.

Tom Cruise was regularly bullied in the 15 different school that he attended in 12 years.

Reference: (http://www.celebritybeliefs.com/tom-cruise/)

410.

In 2005, Facebook hired graffiti artist David Choe to paint murals in their new office space. Choe accepted Facebook shares instead of a small cash payment of several thousand dollars, and when Facebook went public in 2012, his payment for the murals ballooned into a 200 million dollar payoff.

Reference: (http://www.nytimes.com/2012/02/02/technology/for-founders-to-decorators-facebook-riches.html)

411.

Cuba has a vast no-Internet file-sharing network with terabytes of regularly updated movies, television, music, and software delivered by USB drivers over sneakernet for $2 per week subscription fees.

Reference: (http://www.vox.com/2015/9/21/9352095/netflix-cuba-paquete-internet)

412.

During the 2008 world hops shortage, the Samuel Adams brewery shared 20,000 pounds of their excess hops with 108 different craft breweries, at cost, to help prevent them from going out of business.

Reference:(http://en.wikipedia.org/w/index.php?title=Samuel_Adams_%28beer%29#2008_hops_shortage)

413.

U.K. scientists discovered 3 new species of mushroom after buying dried porcini mushrooms from a local grocery store and testing them.

Reference: (http://firstwefeast.com/eat/scientists-discover-3-new-species-of-edible-mushrooms/)

414.

The Russian made Mosin-Nagant rifle, despite originally having been made in 1893, has shown up in various conflicts around the world until the modern day due to being plentiful, cheap, rugged and effective, much like the AK-47, which eventually replaced it.

Reference:
(https://en.wikipedia.org/wiki/Mosin%E2%80%93Nagant)

415.

When Marlon Brando was studying to become an actor in New York, a teacher instructed his class to act like chickens, and added that a nuclear bomb was about to fall on them. Most of the class clucked and ran around wildly, but Brando sat calmly and pretended to lay an egg. Asked by Adler why he had chosen to react this way, he said, "I'm a chicken – What do I know about bombs?" Brando is hailed for bringing realism to film acting.

Reference: (http://en.wikipedia.org/wiki/Marlon_Brando)

416.

A wealthy Canadian lawyer gave $9 million dollars to the mother who had the most children in the Toronto area in the 10 years after his death.

Reference: (http://fivethirtyeight.com/features/how-a-dead-millionaire-convinced-dozens-of-women-to-have-as-many-babies-as-possible/)

417.

In 1860s San Francisco, two stray dogs, who were best friends, became local celebrities. Their exploits were celebrated in local papers and they were granted immunity from the city's dog catchers.

Reference: (http://en.wikipedia.org/wiki/Bummer_and_Lazarus)

418.

A man who attempted to commit suicide changed his mind at the last minute, resulting in a chain reaction train wreck killing 11. He was later sentenced to 11 consecutive life sentences.

Reference:
(http://en.wikipedia.org/wiki/2005_Glendale_train_crash)

419.

There's a bird, called Maleo, that lays its eggs deep into warm sand, allowing solar or volcanic heat to incubate them. The young birds dig their way out and are ready to fly directly after.

Reference: (https://en.wikipedia.org/wiki/Maleo)

420.

The creator of Dungeons & Dragons was a practicing Jehovah's Witness. He would go door-to-door and he would give out pamphlets.

Reference: (http://www.newyorker.com/books/page-turner/the-tangled-cultural-roots-of-dungeons-dragons)

421.

The first proper cinematic use of a bluescreen was in The Thief of Bagdad, which won the Academy Award for Visual Effects that year.

Reference: (https://en.wikipedia.org/wiki/Chroma_key#History)

422.

Paula Abdul choreographed the piano scene in BIG.

Reference:(https://en.wikipedia.org/wiki/Paula_Abdul#1982.E2.80.9 31986:_Dance_and_choreography_era)

423.

Designers wanted their models to look like they were on heroin in the mid-1990s. The look, characterized by pale skin, dark circles underneath the eyes and angular bone structure, was a reaction against the "healthy" and vibrant look of models such as Cindy Crawford and Claudia Schiffer.

Reference: (http://en.wikipedia.org/wiki/Heroin_chic)

424.

Apple created a clothing line in 1986.

Reference: (http://mashable.com/2012/06/13/apple-80s-clothing/)

425.

During the French Revolution, leaders tried to replace Christianity with the "Cult of Reason." Notre Dame Cathedral and other churches became "Temples of Reason," but many reports of "lurid depravities" occurring at them increased opposition to the revolution. Napoleon banned the cult.

Reference: (https://en.wikipedia.org/wiki/Cult_of_Reason)

426.

In 1969, the United States, under Richard Nixon, went into a nuclear readiness alert and flew nuclear armed bombers along Soviet airspace for three days. This was part of Nixon's "Madman Theory," in which he tried to give off the image that he was unstable so that Soviet bloc nations would never provoke the United States.

Reference: (https://en.wikipedia.org/wiki/Madman_theory)

427.

In 1996, when a man was arrested for wearing a Medal of Honor he did not earn, a judge forced him to write an apology letter to all living Medal of Honor recipients as punishment.

Reference: (http://en.wikipedia.org/wiki/Medal_of_Honor)

428.

Jean-Paul Sartre hallucinated crabs his whole life.

Reference: (http://www.critical-theory.com/9-insane-stories-from-the-lives-of-famous-existentialists/)

429.

Dead people were photographed in creepy posed positions to make them seem alive during the Victorian era.

Reference: (http://blubabalu.blogspot.ca/2011/06/strike-pose-postmortem-photography.html)

430.

The tailbone, the appendix, and 'goose bumps' are all examples of human vestigiality, or traits that occur in humans which have lost their function through evolution. The tailbone is the remnant of a lost tail, the appendix was used for digestive purposes, and 'goose bumps' would flare body hair as a defense mechanism or to keep warm.

Reference: (http://en.wikipedia.org/wiki/Human_vestigiality)

431.

In 2009, a bird took down the Large Hadron Collider by dropping a baguette on it.

Reference:
(http://www.theregister.co.uk/2009/11/05/lhc_bread_bomb_dump_incident/)

432.

A Jehovah's Witness was temporarily incapacitated following a car accident. Her doctor transfused her with blood which saved her life, despite knowing she had signed a card requesting this not be done. Following her recovery she successfully sued the doctor for battery.

Reference:(http://en.wikibooks.org/wiki/Jehovah%27s_Witness_Informed_Consent#Drawing_on_the_Jehovah.E2.80.99s_Witnesses_Experience)

433.

Preventing an abort of the Apollo 11 mission has been attributed to the work of Margaret Hamilton, the lead flight software designer for Project Apollo. She was 31 when the lunar module landed on the moon, running her code, and is credited for coining the term "software engineering".

Reference:
(http://en.wikipedia.org/wiki/Margaret_Hamilton_%28scientist%29#Apollo_11)

434.

The expression, "don't assume malice when stupidity explains it," is known as Hanlon's Razor.

Reference: (https://en.wikipedia.org/wiki/Hanlon%27s_razor)

435.

Donald Trump proposed a onetime tax on the wealthiest 1% to eliminate the national debt.

Reference:
(http://edition.cnn.com/ALLPOLITICS/stories/1999/11/09/trump.rich/index.html)

436.

In 1854, during the Crimean War, the British hospital in Constantinople was extremely unhygienic. Patients lay in their own excrement, and rodents and bugs scurried past them. More soldiers died of disease than injury. Florence Nightingale fixed this by getting patients to clean the hospital.

Reference: (http://www.history.com/topics/womens-history/florence-nightingale)

437.

One of the reasons we mount horses from mainly the left side dates back to the ancient times when horses were used as war mounts. Soldiers carry their swords on the left side, to reach with their right hand, and so they could only mount from the left or they would sit on their sword.

Reference: (http://cha-ahse.org/store/pages/151/WHY-DO-WE-MOUNT-FROM-THE-LEFT%3F.html)

438.

One of the Popes was a complete accident. In the Middle Ages, cardinals would often vote a random candidate on the first papal ballot in order to see how the other cardinals were leaning, but in 1334, this backfired when they all voted for the same person: the very surprised, Pope Benedict XII.

Reference:(http://en.wikipedia.org/wiki/Pope_Benedict_XII#Fournier.27s_accession_to_the_Papacy)

439.

Men in the senate aren't allowed to wear anything else but a suit, despite the loosening of restriction of the women's dress code in 1993.

Reference: (https://www.washingtonpost.com/blogs/reliable-source/post/barney-frank-whats-the-house-floor-dress-code-anyway/2011/12/20/gIQAofep7O_blog.html)

440.

Paul Verhoeven, the director of "Robocop" and "Total Recall" never read the book "Starship Troopers" before making a movie based on it because he found it "boring."

Reference:
(https://en.wikipedia.org/wiki/Starship_Troopers_%28film%29)

441.

The creator of Ziggy trained his son to take over the strip by drawing Ziggy into a predicament, such as falling into a hole, and having his son draw the rescue.

Reference: (http://www.nytimes.com/2011/09/21/arts/tom-wilson-cartoonist-behind-ziggy-dies-at-80.html?_r=0)

442.

A study by an American University found that the Toyota Camry and the Honda Accord both contain more domestic content than the "American" Chevrolet Camaro.

Reference: (http://www.carsdirect.com/automotive-news/cities-that-drive-the-most--and-least--american-cars)

443.

Placentophagy is the consumption of the raw, cooked, or dried placenta, under the notion that it conveys health benefits for the baby and the mother.

Reference: (http://www.webmd.com/baby/should-i-eat-my-placenta)

444.

Nancy Reagan regularly consulted an astrologer, effectively allowing an astrologer to have influence over the President of the United States.

Reference:
(https://en.wikipedia.org/wiki/Nancy_Reagan#Influence_in_the_White_House)

445.

In his midget season, 10 year old Wayne Gretzky tallied 378 goals and 139 assists in just 85 games. That is 4.4 goals, and 1.6 assists per game.

Reference: (http://en.wikipedia.org/wiki/Wayne_Gretzky)

446.

Magellan didn't circumnavigate the globe, but he came very close. When he was travelling east, he reached Malaysia in 1511. During his famous westward expedition, he died in the Philippines in 1521.

Reference:
(https://en.wikipedia.org/wiki/Ferdinand_Magellan#Early_life_and_t
ravels)

447.

Oil spread over water can become as thin as a few hundred nanometers.

Reference: (http://www.phrases.org.uk/meanings/288150.html)

448.

If the Hoover Dam's 3.25 million cubic yards of concrete was poured all at once, it would have taken 125 years to cool.

Reference: (http://zidbits.com/2013/05/how-long-will-the-hoover-dam-last/)

449.

An Australian politician once made a speech that was verbatim the same as the one made by Michael Douglas in the film "The American President."

Reference: (https://www.youtube.com/watch?v=HE-AF78jH2g)

450.

In 1948, people believed that a 15 foot tall penguin existed. Zoologist Ivan Sanderson participated and claimed that it wasn't a hoax. However, it turned out to be Tony Signori stomping around in

the sand wearing 30 pound, 3 toed lead shoes as a prank that lasted
10 years.

Reference: (http://mentalfloss.com/article/52460/strange-states-
floridas-giant-penguin)

451.

New Zealand is one of only 6 countries in the world that have never
defaulted on their debt.

Reference: (https://www.bondvigilantes.com/blog/2010/02/02/what-
happened-the-last-time-the-uk-defaulted/)

452.

Piezoelectricity, the electric energy exerted from crystals under
stress, has been shown to significantly increase successful
fertilization in completely infertile couples when paired with
standard sperm injection procedures.

Reference: (http://www.omicsonline.org/open-access/the-effect-of-
piezoelectric-stimulation-in-patients-with-low-fertilization-potential-
2161-0436.1000122.pdf)

453.

Airline captains can arrange special landings to allow the families of
deceased U.S. soldiers to see them as they're unloaded.

Reference: (http://feelsdaily.com/flight-attendant-gives-pilot-
devastating-news-his-response-moved-all-the-passengers-to-tears/)

454.

Researchers are still not sure why humans tend to twitch while
drifting off to sleep.

Reference: (http://mentalhealthdaily.com/2015/05/19/what-are-
hypnagogic-jerks-twitches-before-sleep/)

455.

A city in New Mexico renamed itself "Truth or Consequences" to win a chance at a radio quiz show airing its 10th anniversary celebration from the city.

Reference:
(https://en.wikipedia.org/wiki/Truth_or_Consequences,_New_Mexico)

456.

Cookies came from bakers making small "test cakes" to test the temperature of wood-fired ovens.

Reference:
(http://whatscookingamerica.net/History/CookieHistory.htm)

457.

Bob Marley's "No Woman No Cry" is actually titled "No Woman Nuh Cry". This translates to "No Woman Don't Cry" and it's a comfort song for a woman, not a comfort song for men with no woman.

Reference: (http://en.wikipedia.org/wiki/No_Woman,_No_Cry)

458.

People make artistic sculptures by pouring molten aluminum inside fire ant hills, while the ants are still inside.

Reference: (https://www.youtube.com/watch?v=-IzZMzNfUT0)

459.

Approximately 90% of plague cases in the United States from 1944 to 1993 occurred in four states: Arizona, California, Colorado and New Mexico.

Reference:
(http://www.cdc.gov/mmwr/preview/mmwrhtml/00026077.htm)

460.

Researchers in Tokyo have developed a mirror that tweaks the viewer's reflection in real-time to make it look like they're smiling. The projected application for this tech is for use in shopping mall bathrooms, in hopes that happier shoppers will buy more.

Reference:(http://www.slate.com/blogs/xx_factor/2013/08/07/incend iary_reflection_mirrors_make_you_look_happier_than_you_are_so_ you.html)

461.

Harriet Tubman was a Civil War spy and the only woman to successfully lead an army through the raid at Combahee Ferry.

Reference:
(https://www.youtube.com/watch?v=VpTf1GFjCd8&feature=youtu. be)

462.

During World War I, Harry Houdini threw himself into the war effort, selling war bonds and teaching American soldiers how to free themselves from German handcuffs.

Reference: (http://www.wildabouthoudini.com/p/houdini-biography.html)

463.

A RAF pilot accidentally took off with a woman sitting on the tail of the aircraft. After a brief flight, the aircraft, pilot and "passenger" landed safely.

Reference: (http://en.wikipedia.org/wiki/RAF_Hibaldstow#History)

464.

Certain parts of the world call all sodas "Coke."

Reference:
(https://en.wikipedia.org/wiki/Names_for_soft_drinks_in_the_Unite
d_States)

465.

According to the U.S. Flag Code: "The flag should never be used as
wearing apparel, bedding, or drapers," and: "No part of the flag
should ever be used as a costume or athletic uniform".

Reference: (http://en.wikipedia.org/wiki/Flag_of_the_United_States)

466.

It is estimated that 1,000,000 animals are killed on roads in the
United States every single day.

Reference:
(https://en.wikipedia.org/wiki/Roadkill#Distribution_and_abundance
)

467.

There is a Forbes Fictional 15, which keeps track of the 15 richest
people in the realm of fiction.

Reference: (https://en.wikipedia.org/wiki/Forbes_Fictional_15)

468.

Ricky "The Dragon" Steamboat wrestled by that name because it
matched his good guy character better than his real name, which was
Rick Blood.

Reference:(https://en.wikipedia.org/wiki/Ricky_Steamboat#Champi
onship_Wrestling_from_Florida_.281976.E2.80.931977.29)

469.

It costs $200 dollars to manufacture an iPhone.

Reference: (http://time.com/3426087/apple-iphone-6-cost/)

470.

Wim Hof, a Dutch man who holds the record for the longest ice bath, has run a marathon in Finland wearing only shorts. He also has the ability to regulate his own immune system.

Reference: (https://en.wikipedia.org/wiki/Wim_Hof)

471.

The fastest roller coaster in the world, Formula Rossa in Abu Dhabi, accelerates from standstill to 97 KMH in 2 seconds, reaching a maximum speed of 240 KMH. Air speeds are so high that riders must wear protective eye goggles.

Reference: (http://www.bbc.co.uk/news/world-middle-east-11620485)

472.

In 2012, the White House responded to a petition to have a Death Star built by stating that "the Administration does not support blowing up planets" and that it would not fund a weapon "with a fundamental flaw that can be exploited by a one man starship."

Reference:
(http://en.wikipedia.org/wiki/Death_Star#White_House_petition)

473.

"Slans" was a term that science fiction fans call themselves to indicate their belief that they are intellectually superior to non-fans.

Reference:
(https://en.wikipedia.org/wiki/Slan#.22Fans_are_slans.22)

474.

The actors who played R2-D2 and C-3PO on "Star Wars", hated each other. The man who played C-3PO once told the other man, "I don't do many of these conventions - go away little man," when he was asked to go on tour.

Reference: (http://gizmodo.com/the-men-inside-of-r2-d2-and-c-3po-actually-hated-each-o-1571528684)

475.

The idea of having the Olympic torch run from ancient Olympia to the host country was invented for the 1936 Berlin Summer Games.

Reference:
(http://en.wikipedia.org/wiki/1936_Summer_Olympics#History)

476.

A form of HD VHS called "D-VHS" was released in 1998.

Reference: (https://en.wikipedia.org/wiki/D-VHS)

477.

The largest object in the known universe is over 10,000,000,000 light years across and theoretically shouldn't exist.

Reference: (http://www.huffingtonpost.com/2014/05/27/biggest-thing-in-universe-video_n_5365111.html)

478.

In 2008 in New Jersey, more than 30 officers, including SWAT team members, were engaged in a standoff with a non - responsive supposed bank robber for over an hour before realizing "she" was a cardboard cut - out.

Reference: (http://www.nbclosangeles.com/news/weird/Cardboard-Bank-Robber-Holds-Off-SWAT-for-Hours.html)

479.

2 days before the official "babylift" project, which aimed to get war-orphaned children out of Vietnam, there was a first flight out, with 57 children on board a World Airways DC-8 cargo plane. Because the World Airways flight wasn't sanctioned, it didn't have clearance to take off, and did so in the dark.

Reference: (http://www.npr.org/2015/04/28/402562381/two-days-before-operation-babylift-57-children-were-evacuated-to-the-u-s)

480.

The Ebola Virus wiped out 70% to 95% of the 20,000 gorillas in Congo's d'Odzala National Park between 2003 and 2005.

Reference: (http://www.bbc.com/travel/feature/20130117-gorilla-spotting-in-the-republic-of-congo)

481.

After World War II, approximately 7 million Germans were expelled from the area that is now a part of Poland.

Reference:(https://en.wikipedia.org/wiki/Flight_and_expulsion_of_Germans_(1944%E2%80%9350))

482.

Ori, who was a dwarf member of Thorin and company from the Hobbit, was also in the Fellowship of the Ring. He is the corpse that Gandalf takes the Book of Mazarbul from in the Mines of Moria in Balin's Tomb.

Reference: (http://lotr.wikia.com/wiki/Ori)

483.

As a teenager, Puccini stole organ pipes from his town's cathedral and sold them to buy cigarettes. As the church organist, he rearranged the music to avoid playing the missing notes.

Reference:(http://books.google.co.uk/books?id=0k6oAwAAQBAJ&pg=PT7&lpg=PT7&dq=%22dextrous+enough+as+a+musician%22&source=bl&ots=c0Lmdt12LK&sig=XCxSy380SEcv66w_yGqJcMJWIwU&hl=en&sa=X&ei=SBTUU8GPJoLG7AaOuIHgBQ&redir_esc=y#v=onepage&q=%22dextrous%20enough%20as%20a%20musician%22&f=false)

484.

The phrase, "fight like a girl," is trademarked by a company called TSDC, LLD.

Reference: (http://www.trademarks411.com/marks/86391464-fight-like-a-girl)

485.

While Italy was under the rule of Mussolini and the Fascists, another Fascist regime appeared on its border within a year, the San Marino Fascists.

Reference:
(https://en.wikipedia.org/wiki/Sammarinese_Fascist_Party)

486.

When "That 70s Show" started, the directors required all actors to be 18 or older. Mila Kunis, 14 at the time, told the casting directors she would be 18 but did not say when. Ashton Kutcher, Kunis' boyfriend in the show, was 20 years old at that time.

Reference: (http://en.wikipedia.org/wiki/Mila_Kunis#Career)

487.

In the 1970s InterVision Song Contest, the Communist equivalent to Eurovision, viewers would vote by turning on lights at a given moment; power plants would measure the load to help determine the winner.

Reference: (https://en.wikipedia.org/wiki/Intervision_Song_Contest)

488.

Three Alcatraz escapees used fake heads of plaster, paint and human hair in their beds to fool night guards. They then made a drill using a vacuum motor to loosen air vents, built a raft from over 50 raincoats, paddles with a musical instrument, and a fake bolt made from soap to close their escape hatch.

Reference:
(https://www.fbi.gov/news/stories/2007/june/alcatraz_060807)

489.

There is a possibility that the first person to set foot on Antarctica was a survivor of a shipwreck.

Reference: (https://en.wikipedia.org/wiki/San_Telmo_(ship))

490.

In 1945, a B-25 bomber pilot crashed into the Empire State Building's elevator shaft, snapping the cable. By the time the carriage reached the bottom, a thousand feet of cable had piled up beneath it acting like a spring, which allowed the lone occupant in the car to escape injured but alive.

Reference: (http://www.newyorker.com/magazine/2008/04/21/up-and-then-down?currentPage=all)

491.

Three Alcatraz escapees used fake heads of plaster, paint and human hair in their beds to fool night guards. They then made a drill using a vacuum motor to loosen air vents, built a raft from over 50 raincoats, paddles with a musical instrument, and a fake bolt made from soap to close their escape hatch.

Reference:
(https://www.fbi.gov/news/stories/2007/june/alcatraz_060807)

492.

In 1972, in Gabon, Africa, a natural nuclear fission reactor was created when a uranium rich mineral deposit became inundated with groundwater.

Reference:(http://mragheb.com/NPRE%20402%20ME%20405%20 Nuclear%20Power%20Engineering/Natural%20%20Nuclear%20Re actors,%20The%20Oklo%20Phenomenon.pdf)

493.

A man was sentenced to 20 hours of Beethoven after being caught for playing rap music too loud, as an alternative to a full fine. He only lasted 15 minutes before leaving.

Reference:
(http://www.nbcnews.com/id/27099954/?GT1=43001#.VIh6HXtNv SL)

494.

The Finnish Museum of Natural History in Helsinki has had a Chilean Recluse spider infestation since the 1960s.

Reference: (http://www.bbc.com/future/story/20160413-the-museum-filled-with-poisonous-spiders-that-just-wont-die?ocid=global_future_rss)

495.

The F-117A stealth fighter shot down by the Serbians in 1999 was picked up on radar because it had opened its internal bomb doors.

The open doors increased its radar profile, allowing a SAM missile crew to get a lock on.

Reference: (https://en.wikipedia.org/wiki/Lockheed_F-117_Nighthawk)

496.

In 1970, there were half as many people in the world as there are now.

Reference: (http://www.worldometers.info/world-population/)

497.

Somebody played a pirated movie on a plane, only to find the lead actress in the seat next to him.

Reference: (http://www.mirror.co.uk/news/world-news/passenger-uses-projector-watch-pirated-7113715)

498.

The White House brews its own beer.

Reference: (http://en.wikipedia.org/wiki/White_House_Honey_Ale)

499.

The president of Russian Railways, Vladimir Yakunin, wants to build a bridge across the Bering Strait from Russia to Alaska. This would make a 13,000 mile road trip from New York to London possible.

Reference: (http://www.cnn.com/2015/03/24/travel/trans-siberian-road/)

500.

Your body could be attacked by the new cells in a bone marrow transplant and it can cause chronic issues.

Reference:
(https://www.nlm.nih.gov/medlineplus/ency/article/001309.htm)

501.

Ted's recurring barber shop quarter in the television series "Scrubs" was an existing group formed by the actor who played Ted and they have released two albums to date.

Reference: (https://en.wikipedia.org/wiki/The_Blanks)

502.

In 2009, during a bar fight in Dublin, a man had his hand cut off with a samurai sword. He proceeded to punch his attacker in the face with the stump.

Reference: (http://www.independent.ie/irish-news/courts/sword-attacker-sliced-off-victims-left-hand-26523796.html)

503.

General Anthony McAuliffe, after receiving a threat from the Nazi Army following the Battle of the Bulge, simply responded with, "To the German Commander: NUTS!" The German delegation was only able to translate the message as, "Definitely not affirmative".

Reference: (https://en.wikiquote.org/wiki/Anthony_McAuliffe)

504.

According to IMT-Advanced requirements, 4G LTE technology in phones isn't technically 4G speeds but rather just an improved 3G network.

Reference: (https://en.wikipedia.org/wiki/4G)

505.

An episode of "Peppa Pig" had to be banned in Australia because it taught children that spiders aren't that scary. It was considered too dangerous to teach Australian kids that spiders are not to be feared.

Reference: (http://www.heraldsun.com.au/news/victoria/the-peppa-pig-episode-banned-in-australia/story-fni0fit3-12272183326283?nk=2eca7a78e9934e65b92efef32a3f7943)

506.

A woman who was pulled over for a routine traffic stop, spent 6 weeks in jail because a police officer performed a roadside field test which mistakenly provided a positive result for meth on a spoon she had eaten spaghetti-o's with.

Reference: (http://upliftingdaily.com/10-unbelievable-things-people-sent-jail/)

507.

Aphids reproduce sexually and lay eggs in the fall, but reproduce asexually with live births the rest of the year.

Reference: (https://en.wikipedia.org/wiki/Aphid#Reproduction)

508.

Students who have been in DARE classes are more likely to use drugs than their non - DARE peers.

Reference: (http://content.time.com/time/nation/article/0,8599,99564,00.html)

509.

Some Indonesians undergo pilgrimage to a place called "Sex Mountain" then have adulterous sex there in order to honor a local saint who had sex with his stepmother there but got killed before finishing the act.

Reference: (https://en.wikipedia.org/wiki/Mount_Kemukus)

510.

In 1994, toxic fumes from a dying woman's blood caused an ER to be entirely evacuated, with 23 of the 37 staff sick, 5 of who were hospitalized themselves, 1 of which was in intensive care for two weeks.

Reference:
(http://discovermagazine.com/1995/apr/analysisofatoxic493)

511.

David Bowie doesn't actually have two differently colored eyes, but his left pupil is permanently dilated.

Reference: (http://mentalfloss.com/article/27273/nine-people-heterochromia-and-one-without)

512.

The term "Third World" originated in the Cold War era and refers to the neutral status of nations not directly allied to either NATO or the communist bloc. It is therefore not a financial classification for poor nations.

Reference: (https://en.wikipedia.org/wiki/Third_World)

513.

The Philippines celebrates July 4th to commemorate the day in 1946 when it ceased to be a U.S. territory and the U.S. officially recognized Philippine independence.

Reference: (http://www.gov.ph/republic-day/)

514.

More people are killed in the United States each year by cows than by sharks, bears, alligators, lizards, spiders and venomous snakes, combined.

Reference: (http://www.cnet.com/news/afraid-of-sharks-these-are-the-animals-more-likely-to-kill-you/)

515.

The 1961 film "Victim" about closet homosexuals being blackmailed at a time when homosexuality was illegal. In reality, both lead male actors, Dirk Bogarde and Dennis Price, were closet homosexuals.

Reference: (https://en.wikipedia.org/wiki/Victim_(1961_film))

516.

The castle in Disney's Parks is actually called Cinderella Castle, not Cinderella's Castle.

Reference: (https://en.wikipedia.org/wiki/Cinderella_Castle)

517.

In Oslo, Norway, there is a free medical clinic for undocumented immigrants. They will even provide patients with a translator at no charge.

Reference: (http://www.bymisjon.no/Virksomheter/Helsesenteret-for-papirlose-migranter/English/)

518.

Although adults' health is likely to decline in the short term following a parent's death, the long-term outlook on their physical health is much more positive.

Reference: (http://news.utexas.edu/2003/05/05/nr_sociology)

519.

A custom, 3D printed toothbrush can clean a mouth full of teeth perfectly in 6 seconds.

Reference: (http://www.blizzident.com/how-it-works.html)

520.

Earl Sampson, a Florida black man, has been arrested for trespassing 62 times at the convenience store where he works.

Reference:
(http://www.miamiherald.com/news/local/community/miami-dade/article1957716.html)

521.

A Russian scientists put his head in an active particle accelerator, survived, and continued to complete his Ph.D.

Reference: (https://en.wikipedia.org/wiki/Anatoli_Bugorski)

522.

75% of crimes in the United States are committed by high school dropouts.

Reference:
(https://en.wikipedia.org/wiki/Education_in_the_United_States)

523.

Laika, the first dog in space, did not die peacefully of poison after six days as initially reported, but rather within seven hours of launch, likely due to overheating caused by a faulty temperature control system. The Russians acknowledge the importance of Laika several times over, including a statue.

Reference: (http://en.wikipedia.org/wiki/Laika#Voyage)

524.

The rock band "Pixies" were offered to compose a song for the Shrek 2 soundtrack, but it was later refused.

Reference:
(https://en.wikipedia.org/wiki/Joey_Santiago#Pixies_reunion_and_future_projects)

525.

The pangolin is the world's most trafficked mammal.

Reference: (http://www.iata.org/pressroom/media-kit/Documents/wildlife-presentation-gmd15.pdf)

526.

14 year old Roman Emperor, Bassianus, was one of the most hated emperors in Rome's history. He replaced the Roman god Jupiter with the Syrian sun god Elagabal and was rumored to prostitute himself out in the Imperial Palace. He was killed after only 4 years on the throne.

Reference: (http://www.ancient.eu/Elagabalus/)

527.

In Cuba, picking up hitchhikers is mandatory for government vehicles, if passenger space is available. Hitchhiking is encouraged, as there are few cars, and designated hitchhiking spots are used. Waiting riders are picked up on a first come first go basis.

Reference: (https://en.wikipedia.org/wiki/Hitchhiking#Cuba)

528.

The Oh-My-God particle, a subatomic particle detected to be travelling at 99.9999999999999999951% the speed of light, is carrying the same energy as a 60 MPH baseball.

Reference: (http://en.wikipedia.org/wiki/Oh-My-God_particle)

529.

People with schizophrenia can tickle themselves.

Reference: (http://www.vox.com/2015/3/6/8158211/why-are-we-ticklish)

530.

Moscow State University's math department in the 1970s offered a special test only to Jewish and other "undesirable" applicants. Failing to answer the incredibly difficult questions was an easy way to exclude Jews from the university without causing a public scandal.

Reference: (http://www.tanyakhovanova.com/coffins.html)

531.

According to a UK psychiatry study, 3 out of 11 personality disorders were more common in executives than in criminal psychiatric patients. The business people were described as "successful psychopaths and the criminals as unsuccessful psychopaths."

Reference:
(http://en.wikipedia.org/wiki/Workplace_bullying#Executives)

532.

North Korea once tried to pay back a $10 million dollar debt to the Czech Republic in 20 tons of ginseng.

Reference: (http://www.bbc.com/news/world-europe-10944767)

533.

"Inverted Spectrum" is a philosophy that states the possibility of people agreeing on the names and characteristics of certain colors, though one person is essentially seeing a totally different color. If I have an inverted spectrum, we both say we see a bright blue sky, but if you saw it through my eyes, you could be looking at a bright red or purpose or green sky. Compare to the fact that dogs are proven to have a very limited spectrum of color, humans may also be born with access to a limited or inverted spectrum, and are never aware of it.

Reference: (http://en.wikipedia.org/wiki/Inverted_spectrum)

534.

The Austin, Texas, clock tower shooter left a suicide note saying he felt that there was something wrong with his brain as he knew what he was doing was wrong and couldn't stop it. An autopsy revealed a brain tumor pressing on the amygdala.

Reference: (http://brainmind.com/Case5.html)

535.

There is a widespread but incorrect belief that onscreen portrayals of U.S. Military uniforms must contain inaccuracies to protect actors and producers against claims of impersonating military forces.

Reference: (http://www.myservicepride.com/content/hollywood-make-mistakes-movie-awards/)

536.

In the 1800s, scientists discovered a dinosaur larger than any other animal, twice the length of the blue whale, based on fossil evidence that has since vanished.

Reference: (http://dinopedia.wikia.com/wiki/Amphicoelias)

537.

One out of every 21 New Yorkers is a millionaire.

Reference: (http://www.businessinsider.com/one-out-of-every-21-new-yorkers-is-a-millionaire-2014-7)

538.

The longest straight road in the world is the border of Jordan to Bahrain at 670 miles.

Reference: (http://www.dangerousroads.org/rankings23/3759-the-10-longest-straight-roads-in-the-world.html)

539.

One of the original Siamese twins was a heavy drinker and in poor health. He died in his sleep and a few hours later, his conjoined twin died as well.

Reference: (https://en.wikipedia.org/wiki/Chang_and_Eng_Bunker)

540.

After the attack on Pearl Harbor, Canada was declared war on Japan before the United States did.

Reference: (http://en.wikipedia.org/wiki/National_Pearl_Harbor_Remembrance_Day)

541.

In the immediate aftermath of the Kent State shootings, only 11% of the country blamed the National Guard for the death, while 58% blamed the students and 31% of those polled were indifferent.

Reference: (http://academics.wellesley.edu/Polisci/wj/Vietimages/nolan.htm)

542.

In 2014, South Korean Christians put up a Christmas tree visible from the North Korean border. North Korea responded by calling it a "tool for psychological warfare" and threatened to bomb it.

Reference:(http://www.slate.com/blogs/the_slatest/2014/12/02/north_and_south_korea_differ_on_christmas_tree_decoration.html)

543.

The official academic color for Accountancy in the U.S. is "drab."

Reference:(https://en.wikipedia.org/wiki/Academic_regalia_in_the_United_States#Intercollegiate_colors)

544.

The ability to think of the perfect comeback after the conversation has ended is called "L'esprit de l'escalier."

Reference:
(https://en.wikipedia.org/wiki/L%27esprit_de_l%27escalier)

545.

Paris Metro trains drive on the right rather than the left and its tunnels are narrower than main line ones in order to prevent it from being absorbed into the national railway network.

Reference:
(https://en.wikipedia.org/wiki/Paris_M%C3%A9tro#History)

546.

Marvin Gaye tried out for the NFL's, Detroit Lions.

Reference: (http://espn.go.com/nfl/story/_/id/13464184/marvin-gaye-tryout-nfl-detroit-lions)

547.

DC shoes offered the city of Philadelphia $1 million dollars to unban skateboarding at Love Park.

Reference: (http://articles.philly.com/2011-02-28/news/28637644_1_love-park-skateboarding-ban-dc-shoes)

548.

The acronym for the German Federal Institute for Materials Research and Testing is BAM and German Fireworks get a "BAM Certificate" when they get tested.

Reference:(https://en.wikipedia.org/wiki/Federal_Institute_for_Materials_Research_and_Testing)

549.

The deepest gold mine in the world, the Mponeng mine in South Africa, reaches roughly 2.4 miles below the surface. Illegal miners in the deepest areas stay down for months; the lack of sun causing their skin to turn grey, thus, they are referred to as "ghost miners".

Reference:(http://online.wsj.com/news/articles/SB10001424052702304854804579236640793042718)

550.

Nayakas of Keladi were an important ruling dynasty in post-medieval Karnataka, India. The dynasty also inspired much of the world of CD Project Red's "The Witcher" video game series.

Reference: (https://en.wikipedia.org/wiki/Nayakas_of_Keladi)

551.

Jim Carrey dropped out of high school at 16 to focus completely on comedy and he never finished his education.

Reference: (http://www.imdb.com/name/nm0000120/bio)

552.

East Germany lives on – as a tiny island off Cuba. In 1972, Fidel Castro gifted the island to East Germany. The island was not addressed in the 1990 reunification, and as such is still technically East German territory, even though the nation no longer exists.

Reference: (http://bigthink.com/strange-maps/79-east-germany-lives-on-as-a-tiny-carribean-island)

553.

Congreve rockets fired during the bombardment of Fort McHenry in 1812 inspired the fifth and sixth lines of the U.S. National Anthem.

Reference: (http://www.airspacemag.com/history-of-flight/rockets-inspired-francis-scott-key-180952399/?no-ist)

554.

Japan still has an Emperor, and he is, allegedly, the direct descendant of the first Emperor of Japan.

Reference: (http://www.britannica.com/biography/Akihito)

555.

By peeing in the shower, you can save around 2,500 liters per person, per household.

Reference:
(http://en.wikipedia.org/wiki/National_Pearl_Harbor_Remembrance_Day)

556.

The Pedestrian is a 19th century long distance walker that made a living walking all over the country.

Reference: (http://runningpast.com/pedestrian.htm)

557.

Dinosaur fossils have been found in Antarctica.

Reference:
(http://news.nationalgeographic.com/news/2004/03/0309_040309_p
olardinos.html)

558.

A Canadian Security Intelligence Service employee had top secret documents stolen from his car while attending a Toronto Maple Leafs hockey game.

Reference:(https://en.wikipedia.org/wiki/Canadian_Security_Intellig
ence_Service#Controversies)

559.

The Basque people dominated the whaling industry in Europe for 500 years and were described as "the only people who understand whaling," by British explorer Jonas Poole.

Reference:
(https://en.wikipedia.org/wiki/History_of_Basque_whaling#cite_not
e-MarBarkBark2003-1)

560.

From 1964 to 1973, the U.S. dropped 2 million tons of bombs on Laos. This was enough for a full plane load every 8 minutes, 24 hours a day, 7 days a week for 9 years.

Reference: (http://legaciesofwar.org/about-laos/secret-war-laos/)

561.

At midnight on December 30th, 1899, a ship positioned itself at the intersection of the date line and equator, such that the bow and stern occupied different seasons, hemispheres, days, years and centuries. For this ship, December 31st never happened.

Reference:(http://community.seattletimes.nwsource.com/archive/?date=19900102&slug=1048816)

562.

The ecological effect of eliminating harmful mosquitoes is that you have more people. The issue with more people, is a larger ecological footprint.

Reference:
(http://www.nature.com/news/2010/100721/pdf/466432a.pdf)

563.

Around 10,000 to 30,000 people each year worked to build St. Petersburg as Russia's new capital for Peter the Great between 1703 and 1725, resulting in about 100,000 deaths. It's considered to be the single major engineering project of the 18th century.

Reference: (http://www.spacesyntax.net/symposia-archive/SSS4/fullpapers/17Knoespelpaper.pdf)

564.

A morbidly obese Houston man managed to sneak a pistol into jail by hiding it in his fat folds, before admitting it to the police many hours later.

Reference: (http://www.chron.com/news/houston-texas/article/Gun-found-on-obese-inmate-after-5-searches-1733769.php)

565.

During the Berlin Blockade in 1948, a pilot who was doing supply drops for the civilians became known as "Uncle Wiggly Wings" after he started dropping candy and chocolate from his plane and wiggling his wings so people knew it was him.

Reference:
(https://en.wikipedia.org/wiki/Gail_Halvorsen#Candy_Bomber)

566.

Inner speech, the voice that you hear inside your head when you're reading or thinking, is accompanied by tiny muscular movements in the larynx.

Reference:
(http://www.theguardian.com/science/blog/2014/aug/21/science-little-voice-head-hearing-voices-inner-speech)

567.

Due to the intense mining, Russian city of Norilsk is one of the most polluted cities in the world. Locals are systematically complaining of breathing problems caused by the toxic environment. As if that was not enough, nine underground nuclear explosions for peaceful purposes, including research and mining exploration, were conducted by the Soviet regime. The cancer rates in that area are twice higher than anywhere in Russia.

Reference:(http://weirdrussia.com/2014/06/18/the-city-norilsk-one-of-the-most-polluted-places-on-earth/)

568.

The United States, Germany and France provided samples and equipment to Iraq that served as the basis for its biological weapons program.

Reference:
(https://en.wikipedia.org/wiki/Iraqi_biological_weapons_program)

569.

In 2014, a woman dropped her cell phone in an open pit toilet and 2 people died attempting to retrieve the phone.

Reference:(http://www.cnet.com/news/woman-drops-cell-phone-in-toilet-two-die-in-rescue-attempt/)

570.

In the 50s, one of the major attractions at Las Vegas was watching atomic bomb tests nearby. For a time, Vegas was marketed as "Atomic City."

Reference:
(http://www.pbs.org/wgbh/amex/lasvegas/peopleevents/e_atomictourism.html)

571.

The International Space Station is arguably the most expensive single item ever constructed. In 2010, the cost was expected to be $150 billion. Assuming 20,000 person-days of use from 2000 to 2015 by two to six person crews, each person-day would cost $7.5 million dollars.

Reference:
(https://en.wikipedia.org/wiki/International_Space_Station#Cost)

572.

The rap group "Geto Boys" used an image of one of their members directly after he was shot in the eye by his girlfriend, as an album cover.

Reference:
(https://en.wikipedia.org/wiki/We_Can%27t_Be_Stopped#Album_cover)

573.

After men were exposed to pornography, they rate themselves as less in love with their partner than men who didn't see any porn.

Reference:(http://www.socialcostsofpornography.com/Bridges_Porn
ographys_Effect_on_Interpersonal_Relationships.pdf)

574.

University of Waterloo's Conflict of Interest Policy, regarding
student and professor relationships, is labeled as "Policy 69".

Reference: (https://uwaterloo.ca/secretariat-general-counsel/policies-
procedures-guidelines/policy-69)

575.

The word "Maverick" comes from Samuel Maverick, a 19th century
Texan who refused to brand his cattle.

Reference:
(http://en.wikipedia.org/w/index.php?title=Samuel_Maverick)

576.

Andrew Johnson's pets were mice he found in his bedroom. He often
left flour out for them at night.

Reference:(http://presidentialpetmuseum.com/presidents/17aj/)

577.

Poland's Boy Scout association was transformed into an armed
resistance force during World War II and fought in the Warsaw
Uprising, assassinated SS officials, and liberated a concentration
camp.

Reference: (https://en.wikipedia.org/wiki/Gray_Ranks)

578.

The Norse Sagas which describe the historical pre-Columbus Viking
discovery of North America also say that they met Native Americans
who could speak a language that sounded similar to Irish, and who
said that they had already encountered white men before them.

Reference: (http://history.howstuffworks.com/history-vs-myth/irish-monk-america1.htm)

579.

A woman faced fraud charges after a DNA test showed that she wasn't the mother of her own children. She was in fact a chimera. Those rare individuals, dubbed "Chimeras", had started out as twins; in the early stage of pregnancy, one of the twins had merged with or been absorbed by the other twin. The cells of the consumed twin, however, did not disappear and remained alive in one concentrated area of their sibling's body. In essence, a human chimera is one person made up of two separate sets of genetic material; making them their own twins.

Reference:(http://www.philly.com/philly/news/science/Medical_mystery_Woman_gives_birth_to_children_discovers_her_twin_is_actually_the_biological_mother.html)

580.

Someone using fresh salmon for sushi was infected by many centimeter long worms that were making him sick by chomping their way through the man's stomach lining.

Reference:(http://www.vancouversun.com/health/amateur+sushi+chefs+could+find+themselves+emergency+room/11665422/story.html)

581.

According to the New York Business Journal, the Campbell Soup Co. has recently dramatically increased its marketing budget with the launch of a multimedia ad campaign centered around a boy with a long beard, "The Wisest Kid in the Whole World", who advises people to have soup.

Reference:
(http://www.bizjournals.com/newyork/news/2013/09/10/campbell-soups-new-ads-aimed-at.html?page=all)

582.

St. Lawrence was roasted to death on a hot grill. In defiance he said "Turn me over – I'm done on this side!". He is now the Patron Saint of Comedians.

Reference:(http://ascentofcarmel.blogspot.co.uk/2013/08/why-st-lawrence-is-patron-saint-of.html)

583.

The child from The Shinning, Danny Lloyd, stopped acting as he grew up and went on to become a professor of biology.

Reference: (http://nydailynews.com/entertainment/boy-shining-pig-farmer-science-teacher-article-1.1477838)

584.

Goldfish can have tumor removal surgery.

Reference: (http://www.cbsnews.com/news/goldfish-named-george-life-saving-tumor-removal-surgery/)

585.

Dr. Kelsey, despite immense pressure from pharmaceutical companies, decided not to approve thalidomide for morning sickness in the U.S., saving a whole generation of children from death and deformities.

Reference:(http://en.wikipedia.org/wiki/Frances_Oldham_Kelsey)

586.

Marmorkrebs are an invasive, all-female species of crayfish that can reproduce asexually and whose origins are unknown prior to appearing in the German pet trade in the 1990s.

Reference: (https://en.wikipedia.org/wiki/Marmorkrebs)

587.

Chinese courts have a 99.99% conviction rate.

Reference: (https://www.washingtonpost.com/news/morning-mix/wp/2014/03/11/china-scored-99-9-percent-conviction-rate-last-year/)

588.

Play-Doh was originally sold as a wallpaper cleaner, but with the introduction of washable vinyl-based wallpaper, the market for cleaning putty decreased substantially. After discovering that it was used by nursery school children to make Christmas ornaments, Play-Doh was rebranded as a school supply product.

Reference: (https://en.wikipedia.org/wiki/Play-Doh#Origin)

589.

Since the first atomic bomb was detonated in 1945, over 2000 nuclear weapons have been detonated by 8 different nations in 60 different locations worldwide.

Reference: (http://www.ctbto.org/nuclear-testing/history-of-nuclear-testing/world-overview/)

590.

Demi Lovato and Selena Gomez previously played children on the children's show Barney & Friends.

Reference:
(https://en.wikipedia.org/wiki/Barney_%26_Friends#Children)

591.

The highest grossing single unit independent pizzeria in the United States is, "Moose's Tooth Pub and Pizzeria", in Anchorage, Alaska. Its annual sales are approximately $6 million dollars.

Reference:(http://tondapzza.com/fun-and-interesting-facts-about-pizza/)

592.

There is a tower made out of skulls in Serbia.

Reference: (https://en.wikipedia.org/wiki/Skull_Tower)

593.

Michael Winslow can do over 10,000 voices.

Reference: (https://www.youtube.com/watch?v=61ZEUu0qVT4)

594.

Gaston Glock, the designer of Glock pistols, made prototypes and test fired them with his left hand; if he was maimed by an explosion, he could still draw blueprints with his right.

Reference:(http://online.wsj.com/news/articles/SB10001424052970204257504577149913689465528)

595.

Farmed salmon is naturally gray in color. It ends up pink due to food additive canthaxanthin and astaxanthin.

Reference: (http://www.wired.com/2004/02/the-15-colors-of-salmon/)

596.

The popular torrent website, The Pirate Bay, tried buying their own island in the hopes of establishing their own country with no copyright laws.

Reference: (http://www.factswt.com/did-you-know-that-the-pirate-bay-tried-buying-their-own-island-in-hopes-of-establishing-their-own/)

597.

In 1962, French explorer, Michael Siffre, spent two months in complete isolation buried in a cave below a glacier. His sense of time collapsed but his body continued to maintain a daily rhythm.

Reference:
(http://news.bbc.co.uk/2/hi/uk_news/magazine/4741340.stm)

598.

In May, 1992 Ross Perot was the leading presidential candidate in Texas and California

Reference:(https://en.wikipedia.org/wiki/Ross_Perot_presidential_campaign,_1992#Frontrunner_status)

599.

A man faked his death, lived next door without his kids knowing, fled to Panama with his wife on a fake passport, tried to build a hotel using his insurance money, after a visa policy change he returned home and pretended not to remember anything; his ruse was revealed by a Google search.

Reference:
(http://en.wikipedia.org/wiki/John_Darwin_disappearance_case)

600.

Bullying, child abuse, and stress causes children to age faster at a cellular level and leads to physical and mental health problems even decades later, including an earlier death.

Reference: (http://www.livescience.com/19858-bullying-child-abuse-aging.html)

601.

Trains in Mumbai undergo a "super dense crush load" when there are 14 to 16 people per square meter in each carriage.

Reference: (https://en.wikipedia.org/wiki/Crush_load)

602.

In Vancouver, Canada, exploding a stick of dynamite at a nearby lighthouse was previously used to announce 9:00PM.

Reference: (https://en.wikipedia.org/wiki/Time_signal#Signal_guns)

603.

The baseball from the famous Steve Bartman incident, after being sold for over $100,000, was made into pasta sauce.

Reference:(https://en.wikipedia.org/wiki/Steve_Bartman_incident#Destruction_of_the_Bartman_ball)

604.

The artist Mark Lombardi created visualizations of the financial connections between powerful organizations and people. His last exhibit was destroyed, so he started to repair his works, but before he finished, he suddenly committed suicide.

Reference: (https://en.wikipedia.org/wiki/Mark_Lombardi)

605.

There is an annual gathering of twins in the city of Twinsburg, Ohio. The day is called "Twins Days."

Reference: (https://en.wikipedia.org/wiki/Twins_Days)

606.

The mimicking of an unfriendly counterpart in social situations can cause the observers to unconsciously view the perpetrator as less competent.

Reference: (http://www.livescience.com/15332-mirroring-behavior-downside.html)

607.

Prince used the heartbeat of his unborn son as part of the percussion in one track on the "Emancipation" album. By the time the album was released, his son had died of a congenital birth defect.

Reference:
(https://en.wikipedia.org/wiki/Emancipation_(Prince_album)#Overview)

608.

Cockroaches can make group decisions. When 50 cockroaches are presented with 3 shelters that can only house 40, they'll split evenly into two groups and leave one shelter empty.

Reference:
(http://www.abc.net.au/science/articles/2006/04/03/1607034.htm)

609.

White people in Oklahoma slaughtered up to 300 black people, burying them in mass graves, and burning their town in the worst race riot in U.S. history. This was all done because of a made-up newspaper headline.

Reference: (http://en.wikipedia.org/wiki/Tulsa_race_riot)

610.

Racecar Driver Michael Schumacher Received His Own Private Island from the Prince of Dubai as a Retirement Gift.

Reference: (http://www.autoevolution.com/news/michael-schumacher-receives-7-million-island-from-prince-of-dubai-2604.html)

611.

Only one ship has ever been sunk by a nuclear-powered submarine during military operations.

Reference:
(https://en.wikipedia.org/wiki/ARA_General_Belgrano?repost)

612.

There is evidence that many prisoners were abandoned in their cells during Hurricane Katrina, while the guards sought shelter. Hundreds of prisoners were later registered as "unaccounted for."

Reference:
(http://en.wikipedia.org/wiki/Hurricane_Katrina#New_Orleans)

613.

When one single anti-Kim Jong-Il graffiti was found in Pyongyang, they locked down the entire city for three days.

Reference:
(http://www.dailynk.com/english/read.php?num=7893&cataId=nk01500)

614.

10,000 people follow a twitter account called "Cologne Cathedral" that tweets "DONG" every hour. The amount of "DONGs" shows the time.

Reference: (https://twitter.com/koelner_dom)

615.

The USS Arizona, which was sunk at Pearl Harbor by the Japanese 73 years ago today, still leaks 2 - 9 quarts of oil each day.

Reference: (http://www.nps.gov/valr/faqs.htm)

616.

A 61 year old potato farmer won the inaugural Westfield Sydney to Melbourne Ultramarathon, a distance of 875 kilometers. Almost two days faster than the previous record for any run between Sydney and Melbourne.

Reference: (https://en.wikipedia.org/wiki/Cliff_Young_(athlete))

617.

A father was denied access to see his premature twins in the NICU when Beyoncé and Jay-Z were having their daughter at the same time.

Reference: (http://www.nydailynews.com/new-york/blue-beyonce-special-treatment-bed-stuy-dad-jay-z-turned-lenox-hill-private-club-article-1.1002985)

618.

There's an exoplanet known as J1407. It's a planet with a ring system that is so large that it's 200 times larger than Saturn's. If it took the place of Saturn in our solar system, its ring would be brighter and more prominent than the moon in the Earth's sky.

Reference: (http://www.rochester.edu/newscenter/gigantic-ring-system-around-j1407b/)

619.

The Manson Impact Crater in Iowa was once thought to be the impact that killed the dinosaurs, until it was proven to be too old at 74 million years.

Reference: (https://en.wikipedia.org/wiki/Manson_crater)

620.

Stalin tried to kill Yugoslavian leader Tito 22 times. Tito then wrote a letter in reply saying: "Stop sending people to kill me. If you don't stop sending killers, I'll send one to Moscow, and I won't have to send a second."

Reference: (http://balkanist.net/serbia-and-russia-natural-allies-with-a-divided-past/)

621.

During World War II, President Dwight D. Eisenhower predicted that people would try to deny the holocaust ever happened, and therefore ordered people to take as much photographs of the Nazi crimes as possible, in order to avoid such attempts.

Reference: (http://www.scrapbookpages.com/Ohrdruf/)

622.

A good brakeman, a railroad worker who coupled trains, in the late 1800s was often missing a few fingers, otherwise they were considered a green horn.

Reference: (https://web.stanford.edu/group/spatialhistory/cgi-bin/site/pub.php?id=65)

623.

For two month Ai Hin, a panda living in a Chinese zoo, managed to trick her caretakers into thinking she was pregnant. This was surprising behavior that suggests the bear knew she would be getting extra food and an air conditioned room all to herself. She accomplished this all by just eating more, moving less, and raising her hormone levels.

Reference: (http://edition.cnn.com/2014/08/27/world/asia/china-panda-pregnancy/index.html)

624.

In 1985, the Soviets ended a hostage crisis within 4 weeks by castrating and killing a relative of a Hezbollah leader, then sending the severed organs. A reporter later said, "this is the way the Soviets operate. They do things, they don't talk. And this is the language the Hezbollah understand."

Reference: (http://articles.philly.com/1986-01-15/news/26052630_1_hostage-crisis-soviet-captives-islamic-liberation-organization)

625.

The first dispatch of canisters that were sent through the New York City underground pneumatic mail are: a Bible, a U.S. flag, a copy of the constitution, an imitation peach and a black cat.

Reference:(https://en.wikipedia.org/wiki/Pneumatic_tube_mail_in_New_York_City#Inauguration)

626.

Breathing the air in Beijing is equal to smoking 21 cigarettes a day.

Reference:
(http://ajw.asahi.com/article/behind_news/social_affairs/AJ2013020
30021)

627.

"LES1", a satellite that had been abandoned in 1967, recently started transmitting again, after its batteries decayed, shorting the solar panels straight to the electronics.

Reference:(http://www.southgatearc.org/news/february2013/radio_archeology.htm#.VN4pBy6TeM9)

628.

The Rosetta Stone was a tax document outlining the tax exempt status of a temple.

Reference: (https://www.youtube.com/watch?v=yeQ-6eyMQ_o)

629.

An "ultracrepidarian" is somebody who gives opinions on subjects they know nothing about.

Reference: (http://en.wikipedia.org/wiki/Ultracrepidarianism)

630.

Philadelphia's mayors were initially unpaid, and often strongly objected to being selected - sometimes opting to pay a large fine rather than serve.

Reference:
(http://en.wikipedia.org/wiki/List_of_mayors_of_Philadelphia#History)

631.

According to a study in Poland, attractive people are happier than others but only when they think about their looks.

Reference: (http://sportige.com/beautiful-people-are-happier-only-when-they-think-about-it-92273/)

632.

An average person produces about 25,000 quarts of saliva in a lifetime, which is enough to fill two swimming pools.

Reference: (http://mytempesmiles.com/mouth-produces-25000-quarts-saliva-weird-tooth-facts/)

633.

The baseball legend, Ted Williams, was cryogenically frozen.

Reference: (https://en.wikipedia.org/wiki/Ted_Williams#Death)

634.

"Shashtiamsa" in Hindu astrology refers to the 60th division or "varga" of a "Rasi" or Sign equally divided on half-degree each.

Reference: (https://en.wikipedia.org/wiki/Shashtiamsa)

635.

The sum of all the numbers on the roulette wheel, from 0 to 36, is 666.

Reference: (https://en.wikipedia.org/wiki/Roulette#History)

636.

Alexander the Great wasn't admired much in his lifetime, and was seen by many as a drunken tyrant.

Reference: (http://www.history.com/topics/ancient-history/alexander-the-great)

637.

A clown from Brazil named Tiririca ran for congress. Not only did he win but he was the second most voted of all time in Brazil.

Reference: (http://www.bbc.com/news/world-latin-america-11465127)

638.

Stephen Wiltshire can draw whole cities from memory.

Reference: (https://www.youtube.com/watch?v=jVqRT_kCOLI)

639.

A 27 year old male patient fasted under supervision for 382 days and went from 456 pounds to 180 pounds.

Reference: (http://pmj.bmj.com/content/49/569/203.abstract)

640.

The deepest London Underground station, which went 221 feet underground, was never completed and was used to store secret archives during World War II.

Reference: (https://en.wikipedia.org/wiki/North_End_tube_station)

641.

When Canada loses a soldier in Afghanistan, thousands of Canadians line the bridges along the Highway of Heroes in a show of compassion; hoping there won't be a reason to return to the bridge again.

Reference:
(https://www.youtube.com/watch?v=2eqk0e5J0pM#t=0m35s)

642.

Hans Island is a disputed territory between Canada and Denmark. When the Danish visit, they leave a bottle of Schnapps for the Canadians. When the Canadians visit, they leave a bottle of Canadian Club for the Danish.

Reference:(http://en.wikipedia.org/wiki/Hans_Island#Media_attentio
n_and_continuing_negotiations)

643.

According to VISA, the average American household with teenagers
spent $324 on "promposing," otherwise known as asking someone to
prom.

Reference:
(http://www.practicalmoneyskills.com/about/press/releases_2015/03
31.php)

644.

Municipalities in Liechtenstein, the sixth smallest state in the world,
have a constitutional right of secession.

Reference:
(https://en.wikipedia.org/wiki/Liechtenstein#New_constitution)

645.

During his presidency, John F. Kennedy looked strong, even athletic,
but he was really fragile and in poor health

Reference: (http://www.cbsnews.com/news/cronkite-remembers-
jfk/)

646.

10% of public school children are enrolled in year-round school
systems.

Reference: (http://www.statisticbrain.com/year-round-school-
statistics/)

647.

One of the 4 Lethal Injection drugs paralyzes the prisoner. This
makes their death look peaceful to onlookers, but can hide suffering.

Reference: (http://www.hrw.org/reports/2006/us0406/4.htm)

648.

Leonardo da Vinci may have been half Middle Eastern.

Reference:
(https://en.wikipedia.org/wiki/Leonardo_da_Vinci#cite_note-16)

649.

From 2006 to 2010, excessive alcohol use led to approximately 88,000 deaths and 2.5 million years of potential life lost each year in the United States, shortening the lives of those who died by an average of 30 years.

Reference: (http://www.cdc.gov/alcohol/fact-sheets/alcohol-use.htm)

650.

A hippo must stay moist because if its skin dries out, it will crack. Its skin also secretes a red fluid that is thought to be an antibiotic, sunscreen and skin moisturizer. People once thought that the red secretions were blood and that hippos sweat blood.

Reference: (http://www.livescience.com/27339-hippos.html)

651.

Michael Chiklis was only 28 when he played the middle-aged, retired NYPD detective with a 12 year old son on "The Commish."

Reference: (https://en.wikipedia.org/wiki/The_Commish)

652.

During the Tinku festival in Bolivia, people fight each other until blood is shed. The blood is considered a sacrifice for Mother Nature.

Reference: (https://www.youtube.com/watch?v=apnw7CkY9Qc)

653.

The Blueberry flavor of Jelly Belly was specifically created for Ronald Reagan's presidential inauguration in 1981, where over three tons of Jelly Belly beans were consumed during the festivities.

Reference: (http://www.jellybelly.com/fun-facts)

654.

A pub in Dublin had a strike that lasted fourteen years.

Reference: (https://comeheretome.com/2012/01/02/the-dublin-strike-that-lasted-fourteen-years/)

655.

Jesse James once gave a widow who housed him enough money to pay off a debt collector and then robbed the debt collector as the man left the widows home.

Reference: (http://www.futilitycloset.com/2007/11/18/triple-play/)

656.

John Langley, creator of the TV show "COPS", intentionally shows more white criminals on the show than black ones, despite it being the opposite statistically. He still receives numerous complaints for portraying African Americans badly.

Reference:
(https://www.youtube.com/watch?v=6tLc16_xXlM&feature=youtu.be&t=34s)

657.

In 2007, while in the midst of a home invasion, a burglar lost a testicle after he was struck in the groin by a handicapped man's cane. When the home owner tried to call 911, they hung up on him.

Reference: (http://darwinawards.com/darwin/darwin2007-07.html)

658.

Scatman John had a stutter.

Reference: (https://www.youtube.com/watch?v=K1joxLyd-HA&feature=youtu.be)

659.

A goat was once arrested in Nigeria after vigilantes claimed it was an armed robber who turned himself into a goat with black magic.

Reference: (http://www.reuters.com/article/2009/01/24/us-goat-idUSTRE50M4XT20090124)

660.

Cecil Jacobsen and his wife ran a fertility clinic in the 1980s and he is suspected to have fathered more than 75 children after lies and false pregnancies.

Reference: (http://www.medicalbag.com/despicable-doctors/cecil-jacobson-the-baby-maker/article/472951/)

661.

The chocolate diamond is just a highly marketed, more common, brown diamond.

Reference: (http://jezebel.com/the-truth-about-chocolate-diamonds-5887100)

662.

After Hurricane Ike in 2008, Comcast customers were billed for unreturned equipment that had been destroyed by the hurricane. Customers were charged as much as $1,000 for failing to return modems, DVRs, and other equipment that had been lost or destroyed.

Reference:(http://en.wikipedia.org/wiki/Criticism_of_Comcast#Cust omer_service_after_Hurricane_Ike)

663.

Mark "The Beast" Labbett from the popular game show "The Chase," is married to his cousin who is less than half his age.

Reference: (http://www.mirror.co.uk/tv/tv-news/chase-star-mark-beast-labbett-4421923)

664.

You can't take celery into Chelsea FC's football ground.

Reference:
(http://www.theguardian.com/football/2007/mar/16/newsstory.sport1 1)

665.

Starbucks might have been named "Pequod," after a different Moby Dick character. However, one of the co-founders rejected it.

Reference: (https://en.wikipedia.org/wiki/List_of_Moby-Dick_characters#Mates)

666.

95 year old Li Xiufeng spent 6 days inside a coffin after her neighbor assumed that she had died in her sleep after failing to wake her up. On the day before her funeral, her neighbors were stunned when they saw that the coffin was empty. Afterwards, they found her in the kitchen cooking.

Reference: (http://www.mirror.co.uk/news/weird-news/zombie-gran-95-year-old-chinese-woman-746295)

667.

70% of Americans either hate their jobs or are completely disengaged from them.

Reference: (http://www.nydailynews.com/news/national/70-u-s-workers-hate-job-poll-article-1.1381297)

668.

A shopkeeper tried to assassinate Theodore Roosevelt in 1912, but Roosevelt correctly concluded that since he was not coughing blood, the bullet had not completely penetrated the chest wall of his lung. Roosevelt then went on to give a 90 minute speech with blood seeping into his shirt.

Reference:
(https://en.wikipedia.org/wiki/Theodore_Roosevelt#Assassination_attempt)

669.

Paul McCartney, when writing Eleanor Rigby, named her after a costar and a store, only later to find a grave of Eleanor Rigby near where John Lennon and Paul met.

Reference: (https://en.wikipedia.org/wiki/Eleanor_Rigby)

670.

35% of polled American workers said they would be willing to forego a significant pay raise in exchange for having their boss fired.

Reference: (http://robertehall.com/2014/03/disengagement-economy-robert-hall-huffington-post/)

671.

An office enriched with plants makes staff happier and boosts productivity by 15%.

Reference: (http://www.uq.edu.au/news/article/2014/09/leafy-green-better-lean)

672.

Franz Schmidt, a German executioner from 1573 to 1617, left a diary detailing all 361 executions and 345 minor punishments he performed. The entries contain the date, place, method of execution, name, origin, station in life and the details of the crimes on which the sentence was based.

Reference:
(http://www.americanacademy.de/home/program/past/gods-executioner-meister-franz-schmidt-nuremberg-ca1555-1634)

673.

The first Tour de France winner was disqualified because he cheated by taking the train.

Reference: (http://en.wikipedia.org/wiki/Maurice_Garin)

674.

Scientists in Mexico turned tequila into diamonds by heating a cheap shot to 800 degrees Celsius. At that temp, it vaporized and broke down into its atomic constituents, producing a fine layer of carbon crystal structures identical to diamonds on nearby metal trays.

Reference:
(http://www.theguardian.com/science/2008/nov/13/agriculture-mexico-tequila-diamonds)

675.

A cat named Tibbles was once accused of single-handedly driving an entire species of bird to extinction.

Reference:
(https://en.wikipedia.org/wiki/Stephens_Island_wren#Taxonomy)

676.

Cherophobia is the fear of being too happy because "something tragic" will happen.

Reference: (http://en.wikipedia.org/wiki/Aversion_to_happiness)

677.

In an experiment where a kitten was raised in the same cage as a rat, the cat not only refrained from attacking the rat, but the two became close companions, and the cat refused to chase or kill any other rats as well.

Reference:
(http://www.psych.utoronto.ca/users/shannonian/Kuo/Kuo%20%281938%29.pdf)

678.

The creator of the National Enquirer, Generoso Pope Jr., worked for the CIA's psychological warfare unit.

Reference: (https://en.wikipedia.org/wiki/Generoso_Pope,_Jr.)

679.

The most isolated human being ever was Al Worden, the command module pilot of Apollo 15, who in lunar orbit was at a maximum distance of 2,235 miles from his fellow astronauts on the surface. While on the other side of the moon, no communication with Earth or his comrades was possible.

Reference:
(https://en.wikipedia.org/wiki/Alfred_Worden#NASA_career)

680.

The current BC-AD system of numbering years was first devised by Dionysus Exiguus, who calculated his present year at the time to be 525 Anno Domini.

Reference:
(https://en.wikipedia.org/wiki/Dionysius_Exiguus#Anno_Domini)

681.

There is no historical evidence for any pirate having ever owned a pet parrot.

Reference: (http://qi.com/infocloud/pirates)

682.

The NFL charges the Department of Defense for "paid patriotism," wherein the military pays to provide honor guards for the "Salute to Service" and national anthems.

Reference: (http://www.huffingtonpost.com/entry/defense-military-tributes-professional-sports_us_5639a04ce4b0411d306eda5e)

683.

Changes in CO2 concentration increases the invasive ability of colon cancer cells.

Reference: (http://www.ncbi.nlm.nih.gov/pubmed/23645734)

684.

During the 1963 Philippine Senate Presidential election, Senator Roseller Lim performed an 18 hour speech so that Senator Alejandro Almendras can also vote against candidate Ferdinand Marcos. Marcos won the election due to Almendras's vote.

Reference:
(https://en.wikipedia.org/wiki/Roseller_T._Lim#Political_career)

685.

In 1312, a few Cockchafer Beetles, which were a major pest for crop farmers, were brought into a courtroom in Avignon and ordered to withdraw to designated territory. When the beetles didn't comply, they were collected and killed.

Reference:
(https://en.wikipedia.org/wiki/Cockchafer#Pest_control_and_history
)

686.

Brian May started writing his PhD thesis on the Zodiacal dust cloud in 1971 before beginning his musical career as the guitarist for Queen. He finished the thesis 36 years later, in 2007.

Reference: (http://en.wikipedia.org/wiki/Zodiacal_light)

687.

Switzerland, a landlocked country, has a merchant marine fleet consisting of 47 ships.

Reference:
(https://www.eda.admin.ch/smno/en/home/handelsschiffe.html)

688.

In 1966, there was a white whale swimming up the Rhine River and it's said to be the trigger that began the first environmental movement in Germany.

Reference: (https://en.wikipedia.org/wiki/Moby_Dick_(Rhine))

689.

The Canadian $100 banknote featured an Asian woman on the back using a microscope. People complained that it was stereotyping Asians as being good at technology. She was replaced with a

Caucasian woman, and then more people complained that Caucasians were being favored.

Reference: (http://en.wikipedia.org/wiki/Canadian_hundred-dollar_note)

690.

Looting of DJ equipment during the 1977 New York City blackout contributed to the rise of hip-hop.

Reference:
(https://en.wikipedia.org/wiki/New_York_City_blackout_of_1977)

691.

The ASPCA solved the first child abuse case in America. Since animals had more protection than kids; the ASPCA carried the child out in an animal container.

Reference:
(http://www.nytimes.com/2009/12/15/health/15abus.html)

692.

In 1315, a small change in climate caused a great famine in Northern Europe. The famine was so grim that one day even the king of England was left without bread.

Reference:
(http://en.wikipedia.org/wiki/Great_Famine_of_1315%E2%80%931
7)

693.

In the state of Michigan, you must legally obtain prior written consent to bring in alcohol purchased from another state if it is more than 24 cans of beer or 12 bottles of wine.

Reference: (http://www.michigan.gov/lara/0,4601,7-154-10570_16941-40917--,00.html#a16)

694.

Queen Elizabeth and Prince Philip have been married for over 68 years.

Reference: (https://en.wikipedia.org/wiki/Wedding_of_Princess_Elizabeth_and_Philip_Mountbatten,_Duke_of_Edinburgh)

695.

In the 1940s, a psychoanalyst named Rene Spitz found that it's far better for a child's well-being to be raised in prison by their real mothers than to be raised as orphans in hospitals.

Reference:
(http://phenomena.nationalgeographic.com/2013/07/31/the-orphanage-problem/)

696.

A flipped coin will land on its edge approximately once every 6,000 flips.

Reference:
(http://statweb.stanford.edu/~susan/papers/headswithJ.pdf)

697.

Sharks have been around longer than trees. Sharks appear 400 million years ago while trees appeared 350 million years ago.

Reference: (http://www.smithsonianmag.com/smart-news/respect-sharks-are-older-than-trees-3818/?no-ist=)

698.

Actress Kimiko Glenn was so small as a child that she had to take growth hormones.

Reference: (http://www.npr.org/programs/ask-me-another/481110263/kimiko-glenn-celine-di-on-it?showDate=2016-06-17)

699.

A helicopter pilot landed on the summit of Everest then did it again the next day to prove it wasn't a fluke.

Reference: (http://www.mounteverest.net/story/MysteryChopperlandsontopofEverestMay242005.shtml)

700.

TGI Fridays announced the removal of transfat by 2008, yet in 2016 they still use it.

Reference: (http://nrn.com/archive/tgi-fridays-go-trans-fat-free)

701.

A man was brought to the emergency room with a BAC of 0.37% though he claimed to have no consumed any alcohol all day. Yeast in his stomach was brewing alcohol out of the food he was eating.

Reference: (http://www.huffingtonpost.com/2013/09/18/man-gets-drunk-on-food-without-alcohol_n_3947099.html)

702.

Marilyn Monroe's iconic white dress worn may have been bought off the rack.

Reference:(https://en.wikipedia.org/wiki/White_dress_of_Marilyn_Monroe#Background_and_history)

703.

An Austrian fertility doctor may be the father of up to 600 children due to his obstetrician wife impregnating her patients with his sperm.

Reference: (https://en.wikipedia.org/wiki/Bertold_Wiesner)

704.

"Panorama Blue" is the only known 70 millimeter pornographic film.

Reference: (http://www.in70mm.com/news/2014/blue/)

705.

Kevin Garnett is the Timberwolves' all-time leader in point, rebounds, assists, steals, and blocks.

Reference: (http://www.basketball-reference.com/teams/MIN/leaders_career.html)

706.

Linlithgow, Scotland, has a plaque and museum exhibit to celebrate the chief starship engineer Montgomery Scott, which "Star Trek" scripts state will be born in the town in the year 2222.

Reference:(http://www.heraldscotland.com/news/12781575.Linlithg ow_opens_museum_to_Scotty_who_will_be_born_there_in_the_fu ture/)

707.

Oxford University is older than the Aztecs. Oxford was founded in 1249 while the founding of Tenochtitlan was 1325.

Reference: (http://www.smithsonianmag.com/smart-news/oxford-university-is-older-than-the-aztecs-1529607/?no-ist)

708.

The United States military is using a small turboprop attack aircraft in Afghanistan instead of only military jets.

Reference: (http://www.military.com/daily-news/2016/04/15/a29-super-tucanos-see-first-action-afghanistan.html)

709.

In 2013, The Wall Street Journal discovered a cache of files that revealed the U.S. government lobotomized over 2000 veterans against their will after WW2. The veterans were lobotomized for reasons such as PTSD, depression, schizophrenia, and occasionally homosexuality.

Reference: (http://projects.wsj.com/lobotomyfiles/)

710.

The U.S. National Archive saves all of the presidents' doodles.

Reference:
(http://www.theatlantic.com/magazine/archive/2006/09/all-the-presidents-doodles/305115/)

711.

In 1946, the U.K. created a secret torture program targeting communists, many of whom survived Nazi concentration camps.

Reference:
(http://www.theguardian.com/uk/2006/apr/03/germany.topstories3)

712.

Kamikatsu, Japan's Aspiring Zero-Waste Town, with a population of 1700, has its residents and businesses recycle about 80 percent of the city's trash and only 20 percent goes to landfills.

Reference: (http://www.odditycentral.com/news/kamikatsu-japans-aspiring-zero-waste-town.html)

713.

In October 2014, Amanda Bynes tweeted that her father sexually abused her as a child. She later claimed that this wasn't the case, and a microchip implanted in her brain forced her to say it.

Reference:
(https://en.wikipedia.org/wiki/Amanda_Bynes#Legal_issues)

714.

Native Americans painted lightning bolts on their horses to make them go faster.

Reference: (http://warpaths2peacepipes.com/native-american-culture/horse-war-paint.htm)

715.

Germany is the world capital of penis enlargement, with roughly 8 in 100,000 adult German males opting for the procedure.

Reference: (http://www.medicaldaily.com/penis-enlargement-scene-biggest-germany-does-plastic-surgery-really-work-296042)

716.

In the past 37 NBA seasons, the Warriors, Cavaliers, Mavericks, and 76ers have each won a single title. The other 33 titles have been won by only 7 teams.

Reference: (https://en.wikipedia.org/wiki/List_of_NBA_champions)

717.

Starting in 1938, GM bought out the public transportation in many Californian cities, including Los Angeles, Sacramento, and San Diego, and ran it to the ground so people would have to switch to private transportation.

Reference: (http://moderntransit.org/ctc/ctc06.html)

718.

Saudi Arabia's religious police have an "Anti-Witchcraft Unit" who operate a hotline to which citizens can report magic.

Reference: (http://www.jpost.com/Middle-East/Saudi-Arabias-Anti-Witchcraft-Unit-breaks-another-spell)

719.

Waiters in America pay taxes on the food they serve.

Reference: (https://www.theguardian.com/commentisfree/2013/sep/08/irs-tax-waiter-tips-automatic-gratuities)

720.

A judge sentenced convicted murderer William Hammons to life in prison without the possibility of parole, with one additional term: he must spend every anniversary of his victim's death in solitary confinement.

Reference: (https://www.youtube.com/watch?v=FpynSUaoBdc)

721.

Dubbing foreign films and TV shows into German is a very large industry. More than 40 companies dubbed 90% of the 175 English-language films released in Germany in 2013, each requiring two weeks of work. Some voices become as famous as the actors they dub in multiple productions.

Reference: (http://www.nytimes.com/2014/08/28/movies/dietmar-wunder-the-german-speaking-voice-of-james-bond.html?_r=1)

722.

Russia's only aircraft carrier is so unreliable that it has to be accompanied by a small fleet of tugboats whenever it's deployed.

Reference: (https://medium.com/war-is-boring/your-aircraft-carrier-is-a-piece-of-crap-f3f52d299588#.77r4vg11v)

723.

Seattle has a "tiny house" village that homeless residents can use to sleep, eat and shower. It costs residents $90 a month to cover utilities, and is designed to help them get back on their feet.

Reference: (http://learn.compactappliance.com/seattle-tiny-house-village/)

724.

Gabriel Sedlmayr, a 19th century beer spy and brewery owner, was known for stealing wort and year in a hollowed out cane.

Reference: (http://www.beerhunter.com/documents/19133-000255.html)

725.

Because of a U.S. State Department error, Richard Nixon believed that the Mauritian prime minister was from Mauretania. Confusion resulted as Nixon asking the leader of a jungle country and American ally about desert farming and the importance of restoring diplomatic relations with the U.S.

Reference: (http://www.geocurrents.info/geographical-thought/american-geographical-illiteracy-perhaps-worlds-worst-atlas)

726.

In 1991, a fake Russian TV program on Leningrad TV convinced many citizens that Lenin consumed a lot of psychedelic mushrooms, eventually even becoming a mushroom himself. The Leningrad Communist Party had to declare that, "Lenin could not have been a mushroom," because "a mammal cannot be a plant".

Reference: (http://en.wikipedia.org/wiki/Lenin_was_a_mushroom)

727.

The Ocean Sunfish can produce more eggs than any other known vertebrate; up to 300,000,000 at a time.

Reference:(https://en.wikipedia.org/w/index.php?title=Ocean_sunfish&gettingStartedReturn=true)

728.

Jainist monks are such pacifist that they carry around a ritualistic woolen broom to sweep away insects when they sit or walk.

Reference: (http://en.wikipedia.org/wiki/Jain_monasticism)

729.

Studies show day - to -day happiness increases with income until you hit $75,000 per year. After that, increased income does nothing to increase happiness.

Reference: (http://blogs.wsj.com/wealth/2010/09/07/the-perfect-salary-for-happiness-75000-a-year/)

730.

In 2004, Pizza Hut fired an employee after he shot and killed a robber while on the job.

Reference: (https://en.wikipedia.org/wiki/Pizza_delivery#Hazards)

731.

Richard Kelly, writer of "Donnie Darko," wrote a script that ended up being rejected for a film adaption of Louis Sachar's "Holes."

Reference:
(https://en.wikipedia.org/wiki/Richard_Kelly_(director)#Film_career
)

732.

Timothy Tyler is serving life in prison without parole for mailing 5.2 grams of LSD to a friend.

Reference: (https://en.wikipedia.org/wiki/Timothy_L._Tyler)

733.

Founders of Adidas and Puma were rival siblings who built competing factories on opposite sides of a river. The family feud divided the town for decades. People would often check the shoes of the other person before talking and no dating or marrying would happen across company lines. Some local businesses would only serve Adidas or Puma wearing people.

Reference: (http://fortune.com/2013/03/22/the-hatred-and-bitterness-behind-two-of-the-worlds-most-popular-brands/)

734.

There is no clear definition of what makes a mountain, a mountain, or a hill, a hill.

Reference: (https://www2.usgs.gov/faq/categories/9799/2973)

735.

In 1999, Douglas Adams founded h2g2.com, The Hitchhiker's Guide to the Galaxy: Earth Edition, a "constantly expanding, user generated guide to life, the universe and everything," two years before Wikipedia launched.

Reference: (http://h2g2.com/)

736.

A steelworker today makes five times as much steel per hour as they did in 1980.

Reference: (http://www.steel.org/about-aisi/industry-profile.aspx)

737.

In 2002, 30 British Marines accidentally invaded Spain.

Reference:
(http://www.theguardian.com/uk/2002/feb/19/gibraltar.world)

738.

George Costanza's fiance Susan was killed off on "Seinfeld" because no one liked working with the actress who played her.

Reference: (http://www.hollywoodreporter.com/live-feed/jason-alexander-seinfeld-killed-susan-800031)

739.

In 1864, George Boole a Mathematician and Logician, walked two miles in the drenching rain and lectured wearing his wet clothes. He became ill, developing a severe cold and high fever. His wife believed that remedies should resemble their cause, so she poured water on him, he died that year at 49.

Reference: (http://en.wikipedia.org/wiki/George_Boole)

740.

Mamoru Shinozaki issued 30,000 passes to the people in Singapore during World War II, saving them from being targeted and killed in the Sook Ching Massacre.

Reference: (https://en.wikipedia.org/wiki/Mamoru_Shinozaki)

741.

When Christmas first began, the celebrations included getting intoxicated, having sex, and singing naked in the streets (the origin of modern Christmas caroling).

Reference:(http://books.google.com/books?id=iZ9U0BAV8MwC&l pg=PP1&dq=Ruben+Joseph&pg=PA61&redir_esc=y#v=onepage&q =Ruben%20Joseph&f=false)

742.

George Bernard Shaw sponsored a phonetic alphabet for the English language, with letters like "peep", "roar", "hung", and "ha-ha".

Reference: (https://en.wikipedia.org/wiki/Shavian_alphabet)

743.

Ants can not only grow their own food, but they can also grow their own livestock.

Reference: (http://www.bbc.com/earth/story/20150105-animals-that-grow-their-own-food)

744.

The first child to appear on milk cartons was Etan Patz, a 6-year-old from New York who disappeared while walking to the bus stop in May, 1975. He was never found. However, in 2012, a man named Pedro Hernandez confessed to killing him.

Reference: (http://facts.randomhistory.com/missing-persons-facts.html)

745.

The longest combat sortie ever flown was by the B-2 stealth bomber, lasting more than 44 hours.

Reference:
(http://ww2.dcmilitary.com/dcmilitary_archives/stories/010202/1290 2-1.shtml)

746.

The 1864 Charlottetown Conference, which resulted in Canadian confederation and the creation of modern Canada, was ignored by the local public because the circus was in town at the same time.

Reference:
(https://en.wikipedia.org/wiki/Charlottetown_Conference)

747.

The license plate of Agent Smith's car in the Matrix Reloaded is "IS 5416". This references Isaiah 54:16 which states, "Behold, I have created the smith that bloweth the coals in the fire, and bringeth forth an instrument for his work; and I have the waster to destroy."

Reference: (http://www.eeggs.com/items/40457.html)

748.

Two brown bears were caught performing oral sex in Croatia.

Reference: (http://www.livescience.com/46364-brown-bears-caught-performing-oral-sex.html)

749.

The world's largest moving object, the Bagger 288 Superexcavator, leaves virtually no tracks, even over grass. The sheer surface area of the tracks makes its ground pressure less than a barefoot person.

Reference: (http://en.wikipedia.org/wiki/Bagger_288#Objective)

750.

Richard Francis Burton, an East India Company official, spoke more than 29 languages, translated The Arabian Nights and Kama Sutra into English. He sneaked into Mecca for Hajj, for which non-Muslims are prohibited, in disguise. He was also said to measure the penises of men he encountered.

Reference: (https://en.wikipedia.org/wiki/Richard_Francis_Burton)

751.

When George Washington first ran for the Virginia House of Burgesses, he supplied 164 gallons of alcohol to only 396 voters so they would like him. Washington won.

Reference: (http://drinkboston.com/2008/10/30/vote-independent/)

752.

Elephants, horses, giraffes and ostriches are some of the animals which display homosexual behavior.

Reference:
(https://en.wikipedia.org/wiki/List_of_animals_displaying_homosex
ual_behavior)

753.

Abraham Lincoln refereed cock fights.

Reference: (https://en.wikipedia.org/wiki/American_Game_fowl)

754.

Princess Leonor of Spain has 37 consecutive generations of notable patrilineal ancestors.

Reference:
(https://en.wikipedia.org/wiki/Leonor,_Princess_of_Asturias)

755.

Bull sharks can thrive in fresh water and have been found in the Mississippi river, and as far north as Illinois. This is 1,750 miles away from the Gulf of Mexico, where they're known to exist.

Reference: (http://www.in-fisherman.com/news/sharks-in-illinois/)

756.

In South Carolina, in 1893, a man named Thomas Cherry killed another man with an umbrella for calling him a "damn puppy".

Reference: (https://csidixie.org/numbers/counties/edgefield-county-sc)

757.

After World War I, the U.S. began forced sterilization to prevent "imbeciles" and "promiscuous" individuals from having children in order to clean up the gene pool.

Reference:(https://people.creighton.edu/~idc24708/Genes/Eugenics/History%20of%20Eugenics.htm)

758.

The United States Government didn't declare Independence Day a federal legal holiday until 1941.

Reference: (http://www.history.com/topics/holidays/july-4th/videos/bet-you-didnt-know-independence-day?m=528e394da93ae&s=undefined&f=1&free=false)

759.

Elvis Presley once asked his limo driver, "Do you own this limo or do you work for the company?" He responded, "I work for the company." Elvis said "Well, you own it now." The limo driver's tip was the limo.

Reference:
(http://transcripts.cnn.com/TRANSCRIPTS/0501/14/lkl.01.html)

760.

Over 30 years ago, Buick introduced the first touchscreen infotainment system in a mass produced automobile.

Reference: (http://www.carbuzz.com/news/2016/3/19/Tech-Before-Its-Time-30-Years-Ago-Buick-Put-The-First-Touchscreen-In-A-Car-7732598/)

761.

In Uxbridge, Massachusetts (36 miles southwest of Boston), the local police department has requested that people stop pooping on trains from overpasses.

Reference: (http://www.boston.com/news/local/massachusetts/2014/07/10/uxbridge-stop-pooping-trains-from-overpass/xOGaDzLW51OgPpeiGVbtfL/story.html)

762.

In the Indian state of Uttar Pradesh, many people bribe officials to declare their relatives legally dead, thus gaining ownership of their land. This led to the formation of an organization called The Uttar Pradesh Association of Dead People, to advocate for those wrongly declare dead.

Reference: (https://en.wikipedia.org/wiki/Uttar_Pradesh_Association_of_Dead_People)

763.

Early Chinese MandoPop was denounced as "Yellow Music," which was associated as pornography.

Reference: (https://en.wikipedia.org/wiki/Mandopop#1950s-1960s:_The_Hong_Kong_era)

764.

Bear Grylls was the first person to summit Mt. Everest after breaking a vertebrae. He also was the youngest Brit to summit at 23 in 1997, and he flew over the summit with a powered paraglider in 2003.

Reference: (http://www.chinahighlights.com/tibet/mt-everest/wow-facts-about-mt-everest.htm)

765.

Shaquille O'Neal was a rapper from 1993 to 2001, releasing 5 studio albums and his first, Shaq Diesel, album earned platinum status.

Reference:
(https://en.wikipedia.org/wiki/Shaquille_O%27Neal#Music_career)

766.

The Joystick was invented as the mechanical control for aircraft. The first electronic joystick was patented by an American at Naval Research but the first practical electronic joystick put into use was developed by the Nazis.

Reference: (https://en.wikipedia.org/wiki/Joystick#History)

767.

There's an ice cream that changes color as you eat it.

Reference: (http://sploid.gizmodo.com/scientists-invents-ice-cream-that-changes-color-as-you-1612539292)

768.

Chemist Rudolph Witthaus poisoned a cat with morphine and administered Belladonna eye-drops in front of a jury to demonstrate what a homicidal physician had done to his wife.

Reference: (http://law.jrank.org/pages/2702/Robert-Buchanan-Trial-1893-Grisly-Demonstration.html)

769.

In 2011, Chinese artist, Peiwen Liu, proposed to his girlfriend. But things didn't go smoothly: the girl jokingly told him she would marry him only if he walked 1,000 miles for her. Peiwen took her words literally and set off to walk from the town of Anyang to Guangzhou, a city around 1,000 miles away, where his girlfriend's parents lived. Carrying a backpack and a red flag reading "Eager to meet my mother-in-law," he walked about 25 miles a day. He even started to blog his experiences, which included a terrifying incident in which he was almost murdered by cows. By the time Peiwen was a week away from his destination, his fiancé was already sending him text messages telling him to give it up and go home. When he persevered and arrived in the city, she sent him a text that read "I will not spend the rest of my life with you" and then switched off her phone.

Reference: (http://www.szdaily.com/content/2012-01/13/content_6391720.htm)

770.

The founder of the Schick Company, Jacob Schick, invented the electric razor before 1923.

Reference: (https://en.wikipedia.org/wiki/Jacob_Schick)

771.

Mountain Dew was created to be used as a mixer for Whiskey and the name was slang for Moonshine.

Reference: (http://en.wikipedia.org/wiki/Mountain_Dew#Origin)

772.

Life-sized dolls outnumber people in the village of Nagoro, Japan.

Reference:(http://www.slate.com/blogs/atlas_obscura/2015/03/23/japan_s_nagoro_village_is_mainly_populated_with_dolls.html)

773.

The sharp pain that some people feel on the first steps of an early morning is a symptom of Plantar Faciitis, a disorder in which ligaments on the foot joint have been torn. This is mostly experienced by joggers and runners.

Reference: (http://www.medifoot.com.au/blog/conditions/heel-pain/#plantar-faciitis)

774.

The book series Pippi Longstocking was going to be turned into an anime film, produced by Hayao Miyazaki and Isao Takahata, but when they met with Astrid Lindgren and asked her for permission she denied them permission.

Reference:(https://en.wikipedia.org/wiki/Pippi_Longstocking#Hayao_Miyazaki.27s_cancelled_anime_film)

775.

Quentin Tarantino still owns the "Pussy Wagon" from the movie, "Kill Bill," and drives it around regularly in Malibu.

Reference: (https://www.phactual.com/the-genius-of-quentin-tarantino/)

776.

It's illegal to enter Canada with a DUI.

Reference: (http://123duionline.com/blog/duis-prohibit-entry-canada/)

777.

LSD cured a holocaust survivor from Auschwitz's PTSD and allowed him to sleep for the first time in 30 years without nightmares.

Reference: (http://books.google.co.uk/books?id=H195mY-ZB_IC&pg=PA86&lpg=PA86&dq=Jan+Bastiaans+lsd&source=bl&ots=mgtK5KQNS5&sig=azigPL3CUNKtiG5DxTi0sab1d8g&hl=en

&sa=X&ei=yyrkUs3MK7LKsQT0nIGYCw&ved=0CFMQ6AEwBg
#v=onepage&q=Jan%20Bastiaans%20lsd&f=false)

778.

Mark Mothersbaugh, co-founder and lead singer of Devo, also wrote the theme songs for Pee Wee's Playhouse and Rugrats.

Reference: (https://en.wikipedia.org/wiki/Mark_Mothersbaugh)

779.

The New York Times wrote an article about every single September 11th victim.

Reference: (http://www.nytimes.com/interactive/us/sept-11-reckoning/portraits-of-grief.html)

780.

By 2020, minorities will make up the majority of children born in the U.S.

Reference: (http://www.npr.org/sections/thetwo-way/2015/03/04/390672196/for-u-s-children-minorities-will-be-the-majority-by-2020-census-says)

781.

Creativity has been linked to depression, anxiety, and "madness", with writers being 121% more likely to suffer from bipolar depression than the general population and 50% more likely to kill themselves.

Reference: (http://edition.cnn.com/2014/01/22/world/the-dark-side-of-creativity-vincent-van-gogh/)

782.

Kishi Ryoichi, a Japanese engineer responsible for the construction site of the İzmit Bay Bridge in Turkey, committed suicide by cutting his throat after a cable broke. The site was closed due to heavy winds at the time.

Reference:(https://en.wikipedia.org/wiki/%C4%B0zmit_Bay_Bridge#Accident_at_construction_site)

783.

James Stewart, the math professor whose Calculus textbook is the standard for almost every university in the United States and Canada, died last year, in 2014.

Reference:
(https://en.wikipedia.org/wiki/James_Stewart_(mathematician))

784.

Pablo Escobar's son told a radio station that he would take revenge and kill everyone involved in his father's death. He later took this back and became an architect.

Reference:
(https://en.wikipedia.org/wiki/Sebasti%C3%A1n_Marroqu%C3%ADn)

785.

Surge Soda will be reintroduced in the United States by Coca Cola.

Reference: (http://www.surge.com/)

786.

There is an autoimmune disease which mimics the symptoms of demonic possession, and it has only been identified in the last 10 years. It affects mostly young women and can come on with no warnings whatsoever.

Reference: (http://nypost.com/2009/10/04/my-mysterious-lost-month-of-madness/)

787.

There are more fried chicken restaurants in South Korea than there are McDonald's restaurants worldwide.

Reference:
(http://www.koreaherald.com/view.php?ud=20151005001042)

788.

There is a Buddhist Temple complex in Thailand made out of over 1.5 million empty beer bottles.

Reference: (http://www.sobify.com/strange-architecture-wat-pa-maha-chedi-kaew/)

789.

Adobe Photoshop has origins from Industrial Light & Magic, ILM, and early version of Photoshop was used for creating effects in the movie The Abyss.

Reference: (http://www.creativebloq.com/photoshop/changed-way-we-work-21514234)

790.

A 17 year old kid murdered his parents and hid their bodies in a locked bedroom so he could throw a house party.

Reference: (http://www.rollingstone.com/culture/news/tyler-hadleys-killer-party-20131218)

791.

The Rastafari movement is an Abrahamic religion, in which the followers believe an early 20th century emperor of Ethiopia is the embodiment of Jesus. Among their practices are abstinence from alcohol and unnatural diets, along with their well-known pot smoking and not cutting their hair.

Reference: (https://simple.wikipedia.org/wiki/Rastafari_movement)

792.

The Allied forces of World War II, primarily the U.S., occupied Japan for 7 years after World War II and essentially helped rebuild the country from 1945 till 1952.

Reference:
(http://afe.easia.columbia.edu/special/japan_1900_occupation.htm)

793.

You can exercise your nose.

Reference: (http://www.livestrong.com/article/328861-exercises-to-straighten-the-nose/)

794.

The Titanic's First Officer attempted to "port around" the iceberg, which is a complex task. If he had simply turned the ship, the Titanic might have missed the iceberg with feet to spare.

Reference:
(https://wikipedia.org/wiki/Sinking_of_the_RMS_Titanic#Collision)

795.

A father complained to Target because they kept sending pregnancy product ads addressed to his teen daughter. As it happens, Target was able to determine that she was pregnant based on her purchasing data, which included unscented lotion, cotton swabs and minerals. He later apologized.

Reference: (http://techland.time.com/2012/02/17/how-target-knew-a-high-school-girl-was-pregnant-before-her-parents/)

796.

Photic Sneeze Reflex, sun sneezing, affects 18% to 35% of the population, but its exact mechanism of action is not well understood.

Reference: (https://www.reference.com/science/photic-sneeze-reflex-2440db4e27d374cd)

797.

The first American spy satellites literally dropped their film from space in a "film bucket" that was then scooped up in midair by a plane.

Reference: (https://en.wikipedia.org/wiki/Corona_%28satellite%29)

798.

In the late 1960s, a serving Australian Prime Minister went swimming one day and never returned.

Reference: (https://en.wikipedia.org/wiki/Harold_Holt)

799.

A man had a stroke in 2004, seriously damaging his frontal lobes. He was left with very limited movement on the left side of his body. It also left him with 'the inability to ever feel sad again'.

Reference: (http://www.huffingtonpost.com/2013/08/12/malcolm-myatt_n_3744000.html)

800.

An Australian man had his house burn down in a bushfire only to have a wombat attack him a few days later.

Reference: (http://www.theage.com.au/victoria/manmauling-wombat-felled-by-axe-20100405-rnqk.html)

801.

A 22 year old was shot 6 times in the back in September for carrying a fake katana. Police claimed that he lunged at them which was later heavily disputed by video evidence, however, they got off with no charges.

Reference: (http://www.rawstory.com/rs/2014/11/no-charges-for-utah-cops-who-shot-man-holding-cosplay-sword-six-times-in-back/)

802.

Two Japanese sled dogs survived alone in Antarctica for 11 months.

Reference: (http://www.digitaljournal.com/article/337391)

803.

There are worms that live a kilometer deep in the Earth's crust.

Reference:
(http://www.nature.com/news/2011/110601/full/news.2011.342.html
)

804.

More than 95% of the dogs used in scientific research and testing are Beagles.

Reference: (http://thebark.com/content/beagle-freedom-project)

805.

The reason tendon transplants don't require anti-rejection drugs, like hearts and other large organs do, is because the tendons have been chemically treated to remove "extracellular markers" that cause rejection.

Reference: (http://www.myorthodoc.com/blog/do-acl-allografts-fail-due-to-rejection/)

806.

Pope Pius XII, who is often criticized for not speaking forcefully against Hitler, supervised a rescue network which saved 860,000 Jewish lives; that's more than all the international agencies combined.

Reference: (https://www.jewishvirtuallibrary.org/jsource/anti-semitism/piusdef.html)

807.

July 1st is the national day of Canada, a federal statutory holiday celebrating the anniversary of the July 1st, 1867, enactment of the Constitution.

Reference: (http://www.daysuntil.com/Canada-Day/index.html)

808.

In 1947, Reuben Snodgrass crashed a flying car when it ran out of gas because before takeoff he had checked the car's fuel gauge rather than the planes.

Reference:
(http://en.wikipedia.org/wiki/Convair_Model_118#Operational_history)

809.

In 1928, two Air Force officers flew to a record of 38,000 feet in a small biplane. The controls then completely froze in the -78 degree air, and with oxygen depleting, they waited for 20 minutes until the plane ran out of fuel. Now powerless, the pilot glided all the way down for a smooth landing.

Reference: (http://www.thisdayinaviation.com/tag/albert-william-stevens/)

810.

During the alcohol prohibition, some moonshiners used to wear "cow shoes" which left cow hoof prints rather than human footprints so they couldn't be tracked. The reason this sort of trick worked is because cows pretty much step in their own foot prints when they walk.

Reference:(http://news.google.com/newspapers?nid=950&dat=1922 0527&id=BvtPAAAAIBAJ&sjid=t1MDAAAAIBAJ&pg=3581,695 9265)

811.

Jack White's iconic guitar originally came from Montgomery Ward and was sold for $99 in 1964.

Reference: (https://reverb.com/news/jack-white-and-airline)

812.

President Andrew Jackson served in the Revolutionary War at the age of 13, becoming an orphan at 14 after losing almost all his immediate family to it.

Reference: (http://thehermitage.com/learn/andrew-jackson/orphan/)

813.

Celebrities have to pay $30,000 for their star on the Walk of Fame.

Reference:
(https://en.wikipedia.org/wiki/Hollywood_Walk_of_Fame?wprov=sf la1)

814.

In 2002, the internet was used by Kevin Warwick at the University of Reading to communicate neural signals, in purely electronic form, telegraphically between the nervous systems of two humans, potentially opening up a new form of communication that combines the internet and telegraphy.

Reference: (https://en.wikipedia.org/wiki/Telegraphy#Internet)

815.

The Tarbant, a car produced in East Germany, required that oil and gasoline be poured in and manually mixed by shaking the car.

Reference: (https://youtu.be/T3apze7UYLM?t=15s)

816.

In 1983, a man confessed to his wife's murder after part of a female skull was discovered in a peat bog near their home in England. He was convicted based on this confession. The skull turned out to be from someone who actually died 1750 years earlier.

Reference: (http://en.wikipedia.org/wiki/Lindow_Woman)

817.

On April 18th, 1947, the Royal Navy detonated 6,700 tons of explosives on Heligoland, a small archipelago in the North Sea. It was one of the biggest single non-nuclear detonations in history.

Reference: (https://en.wikipedia.org/wiki/Heligoland#Explosion)

818.

One Hawaiian island is privately owned, inhabited almost entirely by natives who live off the land, and it's largely off limits to outsiders.

Reference: (http://en.wikipedia.org/wiki/Niihau)

819.

Between 1912 and 1948, Art Competitions were an official part of the Summer Olympics, with medals being awarded in the disciplines of architecture, literature, music, painting, and sculpture. Included under "sculpture" was a medal for medal design.

Reference:
(https://en.wikipedia.org/wiki/Art_competitions_at_the_Summer_Ol
ympics)

820.

Irene Triplett, an 84 year old woman in North Carolina, still collects a monthly Civil War pension of $73.13 from the Department of Veterans Affairs. She is the last child of any Civil War veteran still on the VA benefits rolls.

Reference:
(http://online.wsj.com/articles/SB100014240527023036039045794 93830954152394)

821.

Franklin Delano Roosevelt was the longest serving U.S. President, he was elected to the office four times.

Reference: (http://www.history.com/this-day-in-history/fdr-nominated-for-unprecedented-third-term)

822.

The African tigerfish leaps out of water to catch barn swallows in midair. They are a regular part of its summer diet.

Reference:
(http://voices.nationalgeographic.com/2014/01/13/freshwater-fish-leap-into-air-prey-on-birds/)

823.

Yokohama is the largest city by population in Japan.

Reference: (https://en.wikipedia.org/wiki/Yokohama)

824.

As late as 1985, babies were operated on without anesthesia because doctors believed that they did not feel pain. In a shocking case, a pre-mature infant had open heart surgery with no pain relief during the operation. He was also given a drug that left him unable to move, but totally conscious.

Reference: (http://www.macleans.ca/society/life/this-wont-hurt-a-bit/)

825.

A doctor in Australia 3D printed a man's vertebrae and successfully installed the components. Not only that but they were two highly-specialized vertebrae that are involved in the flexion and rotation of the cranium.

Reference: (http://mashable.com/2016/02/25/3d-printed-vertebrae-spine/)

826.

An individual horse has a peak power output of 14.9 horsepower. A healthy human can produce about 1.2 horsepower briefly and sustain about 0.1 horsepower indefinitely. Trained athletes can manage up to 2.5 horsepower briefly and 0.3 horsepower for a period of several hours.

Reference:
(http://en.wikipedia.org/wiki/Horsepower#History_of_the_unit)

827.

The Australian Government went to war against 20,000 emus for one month and eight days using machine guns. In the end, the emus won.

Reference: (https://en.wikipedia.org/wiki/Emu_War)

828.

There are people born without irises which causes their eyes to look black.

Reference: (http://en.wikipedia.org/wiki/Aniridia)

829.

Mt. Kīlauea, a shield volcano, has been continuously erupting since 1983.

Reference: (https://en.wikipedia.org/wiki/K%C4%ABlauea)

830.

When a person dies, hearing is the last sense to go.

Reference:
(http://www.abc.net.au/science/articles/2006/05/18/2809176.htm)

831.

Hawaii's state fish is the "Reef Triggerfish", but the locals call it "humuhumunukunukuapua'a", which translates to, "triggerfish with a pig-like short snout."

Reference: (http://www.lovebigisland.com/quick-and-remarkable-facts-about-hawaii/#Humuhumunukunukuapuaa)

832.

The McGurk effect is an illusion which occurs when visual information a person gets from seeing a person speak changes the way they hear sound.

Reference: (https://en.wikipedia.org/wiki/McGurk_effect)

833.

The corpse flower's binomial name, amorphophallus titanum, roughly translate to giant misshapen penis.

Reference: (http://www.kew.org/science-conservation/plants-fungi/amorphophallus-titanum-titan-arum)

834.

According to many estimates, 1 in every 4 car crashes in the United States is associated with cell phone usage by at least one of the drivers.

Reference: (http://www.nsc.org/learn/NSC-Initiatives/Pages/distracted-driving.aspx?var=mnm)

835.

Highly educated women react to employment uncertainty by postponing or not having children. In contrast, less-educated women often maintain or increase their fertility.

Reference:
(https://www.theguardian.com/world/2011/jun/30/recession-educated-women-postpone-babies)

836.

Several Hells Angels members plotted to murder Mick Jagger after he called them out for fatally stabbing a black man at their free concert in Altamont, California in 1969. They took a boat to his location on Long Island, but had to swim for their lives when a major storm brewed up.

Reference:
(https://en.wikipedia.org/wiki/Mick_Jagger#Hells_Angels)

837.

The Galileo spacecraft remotely detected life on Earth through experiments designed by Carl Sagan.

Reference:(https://en.wikipedia.org/wiki/Galileo_%28spacecraft%29#Remote_detection_of_life_on_Earth)

838.

Mormons believe that the Garden of Eden was located in Jackson County, Missouri.

Reference:(http://en.wikipedia.org/wiki/Garden_of_Eden#Jackson_County.2C_Missouri.2C_North_America)

839.

The parents of balloon boy are still trying to get famous; the kids are now in the youngest metal band.

Reference:
(http://www.usatoday.com/story/news/nation/2014/10/15/balloon-boy-5-years-later/17327017/)

840.

For centuries before refrigeration, Russians dropped live frogs into their milk to keep it from spoiling. Secretions from their skin inhibited the growth of bacteria.

Reference:
(http://www.npr.org/blogs/health/2012/12/17/167255929/scientists-look-for-new-drugs-in-skin-of-russian-frog)

841.

Rory McCann, who plays "The Hound" in Game of Thrones, was fired from his first acting gig for laughing during the takes.

Reference: (https://en.wikipedia.org/wiki/Rory_McCann#Career)

842.

In 2012, Chile made it illegal to include toys with kid's meals. Fast food restaurants kept including toys anyway.

Reference: (http://www.huffingtonpost.com/2012/08/01/chile-sues-fast-food-chains_n_1730756.html)

843.

Adultery in the United States Military is a criminal offense.

Reference: (http://militarylawcenter.com/practice-area/adultery-in-the-military/)

844.

It was once a fashion trend for women to wear rouge, on their knees.

Reference: (http://www.beautylish.com/a/vzvuv/knee-rouge-a-forgotten-trend)

845.

A Jehovah's Witness was temporarily incapacitated following a car accident. Her doctor transfused her with blood which saved her life, despite knowing she had signed a card requesting this not be done. Following her recovery she successfully sued the doctor for battery.

Reference:(http://en.wikibooks.org/wiki/Jehovah%27s_Witness_Informed_Consent#Drawing_on_the_Jehovah.E2.80.99s_Witnesses_Experience)

846.

There is a McDonald's restaurant in Fairbury, Illinois, that was actually open and started 5 years before the chain McDonald's came around, but the restaurant in the small town ended up caving in to the corporation.

Reference: (http://articles.chicagotribune.com/1996-08-15/news/9608150152_1_ronald-mcdonald-corporate-clown-town)

847.

Thomas Baron, a NASA contractor, died with his family when their car stalled on train tracks – a week after he submitted a report (which later was lost) alleging foul play in the accidental deaths of Apollo 1 crew members.

Reference: (http://en.wikipedia.org/wiki/Thomas_Baron)

848.

While acting as a martial arts instructor for Sean Connery, Steven Seagal broke one of Connery's wrists.

Reference: (https://en.wikipedia.org/wiki/Steven_Seagal)

849.

In Ancient Egypt, little people were well - respected and some were considered to be gods. The Egyptians were tolerant of many medical disorders, and they thought that caring for all people was a moral duty.

Reference: (http://originalpeople.org/ancient-egyptians-held-african-pygmies-high-esteem/)

850.

The classic Christmas song "Do You Hear What I Hear?" was written in 1962 as a plea for peace during the Cuban Missile Crisis. The songwriters were opposed to its use as a Christmas song because of the holiday's excessive commercialization.

Reference:
(https://en.wikipedia.org/wiki/Do_You_Hear_What_I_Hear%3F)

851.

"Kuru" was a real disease cannibals could catch if they ate the brains of other human beings. The disease would form holes in their brains and cause them to laugh uncontrollably.

Reference: (https://en.wikipedia.org/wiki/Kuru_(disease))

852.

The Ancient Romans built a fleet of wine tanker, "Dolia", ships. The largest ships carried nearly 50,000 bottles of wine at a time in massive ceramic containers.

Reference: (http://vinepair.com/wine-blog/10-ancient-archaeological-wine-discoveries/)

853.

Ulysses S. Grant's name was actually Hiram Ulysses Grant. When applying to West Point, the senator helping with his application accidentally wrote down the wrong name. Grant's attempts to fix the clerical error with West Point failed and the name stuck for the rest of his career.

Reference: (http://blog.nyhistory.org/ulysses-grant/)

854.

The architect of the Hungarian Parliament Building went blind before its completion in 1904.

Reference:
(https://en.wikipedia.org/wiki/Hungarian_Parliament_Building#History)

855.

The Ebola Virus wiped out 70% - 95% of the 20,000 gorillas in Congo's d'Odzala National Park between 2003 and 2005.

Reference: (http://www.bbc.com/travel/feature/20130117-gorilla-spotting-in-the-republic-of-congo)

856.

A Florida man once called 911 eighty times to demand Kool-Aid, hamburgers, and weed.

Reference: (http://www.miaminewtimes.com/news/florida-man-calls-911-eighty-times-to-demand-kool-aid-hamburgers-and-weed-6559505)

857.

A major tiger reserve in India was found to not actually have any tigers.

Reference: (http://en.wikipedia.org/wiki/Panna_National_Park#Tiger_reserve)

858.

ABC has been cutting scenes from "A Charlie Brown Christmas" to make room for more commercials.

Reference: (http://www.washingtonpost.com/blogs/comic-riffs/post/a-christmas-wish-dont-cut-down-my-charlie-brown-christmas/2011/12/06/gIQAcZ4fcO_blog.html)

859.

Magnum P.I, the original Hawaii Five-O and Simon & Simon all had a shared universe.

Reference: (https://en.wikipedia.org/wiki/Magnum,_P.I.)

860.

Frank Lentini was an Italian showman that was well known for having three legs, four feet and two genitals.

Reference: (https://en.wikipedia.org/wiki/Frank_Lentini)

861.

Some people call Sriracha "rooster sauce" because of the rooster on the Huy Fong label. It's there because Tran was born in 1945, the Chinese Year of the Rooster.

Reference:
(https://en.wikipedia.org/wiki/Sriracha_sauce_(Huy_Fong_Foods))

862.

LeBron James can buy a brand new BMW after working for just 3 hours, while a nurse has to work for over 7 months to earn one.

Reference: (http://www.retale.com/info/salaries-in-real-time/)

863.

Yoda in Star Wars and Miss Piggy in The Muppets were voiced by the same person.

Reference: (http://starwars.wikia.com/wiki/Frank_Oz)

864.

The Oh-My-God particle, a subatomic particle detected to be travelling at 99.99999999999999999951% the speed of light, is carrying the same energy as a 60 MPH baseball.

Reference: (http://en.wikipedia.org/wiki/Oh-My-God_particle)

865.

11 people were killed and 10,500 people injured by fireworks in 2014.

Reference: (http://www.cpsc.gov//Global/Research-and-Statistics/Injury-Statistics/Fuel-Lighters-and-Fireworks/Fireworks_Report_2014.pdf)

866.

In 1876, meat fell from the sky for a few minutes in Bath County, Kentucky.

Reference: (http://en.wikipedia.org/wiki/Kentucky_meat_shower)

867.

Russian and NATO troops were very close to using force against each other in Kosovo, 1999. A NATO commander disobeyed the orders he was given, reportedly saying "I'm not going to start the Third World War for you" to his superior, who was later fired.

Reference:
(http://en.wikipedia.org/w/index.php?title=Incident_at_Pristina_airport)

868.

IANAL is slang for "I am not a lawyer".

Reference: (http://www.internetslang.com/IANAL-meaning-definition.asp)

869.

In the Kent State massacre, of the students killed the one closest to the guardsmen was over 200 feet away, and two of those killed were just walking to class.

Reference: (https://en.wikipedia.org/wiki/Kent_State_shootings)

870.

In 2009, Sandia National Labs booted a supercomputer with 1 million Linux based virtual machines on it to study botnets and how they spread.

Reference: (http://gcn.com/articles/2009/08/10/sandia-botnet.aspx)

871.

None of the paintings Bob Ross painted on air were spontaneous. He would refer to a painting he created earlier that was hidden off camera.

Reference: (http://mentalfloss.com/article/31206/what-happened-bob-ross-paintings)

872.

The word "Maverick" comes from Samuel Maverick, a 19th century Texan who refused to brand his cattle.

Reference:
(http://en.wikipedia.org/w/index.php?title=Samuel_Maverick)

873.

A1 Steak Sauce is a vegan product.

Reference: (http://www.isitvegan.com/2012/05/17/is-a1-steaksauce-vegan/)

874.

Only 8% of the world's currency exists as physical cash, the rest is electronic.

Reference: (http://money.howstuffworks.com/currency6.htm)

875.

North Korea is actually in the top 40 for Summer Olympics medals.

Reference: (http://www.worldatlas.com/articles/countries-with-the-most-olympic-medals.html)

876.

Hitler had a relative called "Paddy Hitler" who ended up joining the U.S. Navy, where, along with all recruits, he had to fill out a form listing any relatives who might be fighting for the enemy.

Reference:
(http://blogs.telegraph.co.uk/news/edwest/100160611/hitlers-children-and-the-sins-of-the-fathers/)

877.

700 Europeans deserted the U.S. Army during the Mexican-American War and formed the Saint Patrick battalion that fought for Mexico.

Reference:
(https://en.wikipedia.org/wiki/Saint_Patrick%27s_Battalion)

878.

Top retailers have price tag codes so if the price ends with .99, you're paying full retail price. .97 is the discounted price.

Reference: (http://finance.yahoo.com/blogs/daily-ticker/secret-price-codes-of-top-retailers-143704248.html)

879.

The Original Oompa Loompas in the book, The Charlie and the Chocolate Factory, were a tribe of Black Pygmies then changed a decade later.

Reference: (http://www.roalddahlfans.com/dahls-work/books/charlie-and-the-chocolate-factory/politically-correct-oompa-loompa-evolution/)

880.

The primary colors are different if you're talking about paint than if you're talking about light. For light, they're red, green and blue. For pigment and paint, they're red, yellow and blue.

Reference:
(http://www.thenakedscientists.com/HTML/questions/question/3361
/)

881.

Will Rogers "discovered" Gene Autry.

Reference: (http://www.cmt.com/artists/gene-autry/biography/)

882.

For two month Ai Hin, a panda living in a Chinese zoo, managed to trick her caretakers into thinking she was pregnant. This was surprising behavior that suggests the bear knew she would be getting extra food and an air conditioned room all to herself. She accomplished this all by just eating more, moving less, and raising her hormone levels.

Reference: (http://edition.cnn.com/2014/08/27/world/asia/china-panda-pregnancy/index.html)

883.

Some fleas in a Flea Circus were glued to a base of a circus enclosure. Miniature musical instruments were then glued to the flea performers and the enclosure was heated. The fleas fought to escape, giving the impression of fleas playing instruments.

Reference: (https://en.wikipedia.org/wiki/Flea_circus)

884.

Sweden offers 480 days of paid maternity (and paternity) leave.

Reference: (http://www.mindflash.com/blog/2012/01/infographic-baby-benefits-is-your-company-offering-enough-maternity-leave/)

885.

Physicists proved that shooting "granny style" is the absolute best technique to consistently score points on the line, but NBA players refuse to do it because it looks stupid.

Reference: (http://discovermagazine.com/2008/the-body/07-physics-proves-it-everyone-should-shoot-granny-style)

886.

In a Fox News interview for Now You See Me, Morgan Freeman fell asleep while co - star Michael Caine was chatting. Freeman responded, "Regarding my recent interview, I wasn't actually sleeping. I'm a beta tester for Google Eyelids and I was merely taking the opportunity to update my Facebook Page".

Reference: (http://newsfeed.time.com/2013/05/23/watch-did-morgan-freeman-nod-off-during-an-interview/)

887.

Thiomargarita namibiensis, the largest bacteria in existence, is actually visible to the human eye.

Reference: (http://wikipedia.org/wiki/Thiomargarita_namibiensis)

888.

Kim Jong-Il was once recorded on tape saying that, "There is a real problem in socialism: no incentive for success."

Reference: (http://nypost.com/2015/01/18/how-north-koreas-dictator-once-kidnapped-stars-to-make-movies/)

889.

Former And1 Mixtape Tour Streetball star "Escalade" was the brother of former NBA player and current ESPN analyst Mark Jackson.

Reference: (https://en.wikipedia.org/wiki/Troy_Jackson)

890.

Nuclear landmines existed until the late 1980s.

Reference:
(https://en.wikipedia.org/wiki/Atomic_demolition_munition)

891.

Investigations into corruption of Victoria Police's Drug Squad revealed a plumber was left alone in the evidence warehouse. He was told to lock up after he was finished.

Reference:
(https://www.ombudsman.vic.gov.au/getattachment/a5c68a7a-f05f-4a0f-a23f-51110f113788)

892.

There is a skyscraper in Los Angeles that is building a slide about 1,000 feet above the ground. The 36-foot-long glass slide will allow thrill-seekers to slide from the 70th floor down to the 69th floor on the outside of the building.

Reference: (http://www.cbsnews.com/news/skyslide-los-angeles-skyscraper-us-bank-tower-building-slide-70-floors-above-ground/)

893.

Paleontologists found fossils of "Machimosaurus rex," a prehistoric crocodile that would have been the size of a bus, 30 feet long and weighing 3 tons. The skull discovered is over 5 feet long, making it the world's largest sea-dwelling crocodile.

Reference: (https://www.washingtonpost.com/news/speaking-of-science/wp/2016/01/12/terrifying-ancient-crocodile-discovered-in-the-sahara-was-the-size-of-a-bus/?wprss=rss_health-science)

894.

When Sydney was decommissioning its monorail, Google purchased two carriages to use as meeting rooms.

Reference: (http://www.smh.com.au/nsw/google-installs-monorail-carriages-in-its-office-20131009-2v7fl.html)

895.

Roman Emperor Constantius II forbade Christian prostitutes from working with non-Christians.

Reference: (https://en.wikipedia.org/wiki/Constantius_II#Christianity)

896.

The bottom of Lake Ontario is so cold that skyscrapers use it as coolant for AC systems.

Reference: (https://en.wikipedia.org/wiki/Deep_water_source_cooling)

897.

Movie producer Mike Todd coined the term "cameo" in 1956 while making "Around the World in 80 Days."

Reference: (http://biography.yourdictionary.com/mike-todd)

898.

PBS released an album where they remixed various show hosts from over the years, one of which was Mr. Rogers.

Reference: (https://www.youtube.com/watch?v=OFzXaFbxDcM)

899.

Currently, there are 86 LEGO bricks for every single person on the planet.

Reference: (http://education.lego.com/en-us/about-us/lego-education-worldwide/lego-facts)

900.

Colonel Sanders was in a shootout with a local rival who killed a bystander. With his competitor convicted of murder, Sanders' first restaurant lost its competition.

Reference: (http://factually.gizmodo.com/no-colonel-sanders-never-killed-a-man-in-a-shootout-1651797965)

901.

35% of polled American workers said they would be willing to forego a significant pay raise in exchange for having their boss fired.

Reference: (http://robertehall.com/2014/03/disengagement-economy-robert-hall-huffington-post/)

902.

Ulysses S. Grant's name was a misnomer, born Hiram Ulysses Grant, the 'S' means nothing.

Reference:(https://en.wikipedia.org/wiki/Early_life_and_career_of_Ulysses_S._Grant#West_Point)

903.

Britain's youngest female murderer is aged 10 and claimed to see the devil every night in her dreams.

Reference: (http://en.wikipedia.org/wiki/Mary_Bell)

904.

While most people associate the 1860s with the U.S. Civil War, it was also a great period of literary publishing with Darwin, Dickens, Carroll, Dostoyevsky, and Tolstoy all publishing books that would go on to be classics.

Reference: (http://waitbutwhy.com/2016/01/horizontal-history.html)

905.

A man fought for nearly a decade to prevent the bank from foreclosing on his home, saying "I'll tear it down before I let you take it." When foreclosure proceedings began, he leveled the house with a bulldozer.

Reference: (http://www.huffingtonpost.com/2010/02/23/terry-hoskins-ohio-man-bu_n_472845.html)

906.

27 million acres of the Amazon have been sold for logging.

Reference:
(http://www.globalpost.com/dispatch/brazil/101019/logging-amazon-rainforest)

907.

In 2010, Sir Christopher Lee released and sang in a heavy metal opera.

Reference:
(https://en.wikipedia.org/wiki/Charlemagne:_By_the_Sword_and_the_Cross)

908.

The origin of the Honeycrisp Apple is a 50 year old secret, known only to the creators.

Reference: (https://en.wikipedia.org/wiki/Honeycrisp#Genetics)

909.

There are at least 18 different ways to tie a shoelace knot.

Reference: (http://www.fieggen.com/shoelace/knots.htm)

910.

The founder of the "Gillette" razor company's full name was King Camp Gillette.

Reference: (https://en.wikipedia.org/wiki/King_Camp_Gillette)

911.

Jet Ski, wave runner, sea-doo and realtor are all technically trademarks.

Reference:(https://en.wikipedia.org/wiki/List_of_generic_and_gener icized_trademarks#List_of_protected_trademarks_frequently_used_ as_generic_terms)

912.

There's an annual lying competition in England, and competitors from around the world have five minutes to tell the biggest and most convincing lie they can. Politicians and lawyers are banned from entering because they're thought to be too good at it.

Reference: (http://en.wikipedia.org/wiki/World%27s_Biggest_Liar)

913.

Many uncontacted people in the Amazon are deliberately hunted down and killed.

Reference: (http://www.survivalinternational.org/tribes/uncontacted-brazil)

914.

In the late 19th century Americans rallied against the metric system because it was an "atheistic system".

Reference:
([http://en.wikipedia.org/wiki/United_States_customary_units#History](http://en.wikipedia.org/wiki/United_States_customary_units#Histor y))

915.

The Mona Lisa was stolen in 1911 and returned in 1913.

Reference: (https://en.wikipedia.org/wiki/Vincenzo_Peruggia#Theft)

916.

In the early 20s, inventor Thomas Midgley Jr. discovered that he could make car engines more efficient by adding tetraethyllead to gasoline, and was awarded a Nichols Medal. Later, it was discovered that the chemicals had filled the atmosphere with lead, leading to worldwide lead poisoning.

In the late 20s, the same inventor synthesized one of the chloroflourocarbons, known as CFC, and received the Perkin Medal. It was later discovered that the immense amounts of CFC produced by hairspray and other everyday products had reduced the ozone layer by 4% every decade since the invention. The wound is not expected to heal fully within our lifetimes.

At the age of 51, Midgley contracted polio. Unable to get out of bed himself, he constructed a machine which could pull him out and help him stand without his family having to help. He got entangled in the wires and died of suffocation. It is now believed that Midgley has affected out planet's atmosphere more than any other organism that has ever existed.

Reference: (http://en.wikipedia.org/wiki/Thomas_Midgley,_Jr.)

917.

Men regularly become erect while under anesthesia.

Reference: (http://www.joacp.org/article.asp?issn=0970-9185;year=2012;volume=28;issue=3;spage=402;epage=403;aulast=Prakash)

918.

Albert Einstein's brain is not actually intact, but it's rather dissected into 240 different cubes that were distributed among researchers for study.

Reference:
(http://phenomena.nationalgeographic.com/2014/04/21/the-tragic-story-of-how-einsteins-brain-was-stolen-and-wasnt-even-special/)

919.

The cave paintings at Lascaux, which depict a prehistoric star map painting that includes animals represented in a zodiacal fashion, have been called the earliest evidence of man's knowledge and fascination with the stars. It's dated at 16,500 years old.

Reference: (http://news.bbc.co.uk/2/hi/science/nature/871930.stm)

920.

Plants can "hear" being eaten and then react defensively.

Reference: (http://www.washingtonpost.com/national/health-science/can-plants-hear-study-finds-that-vibrations-prompt-some-to-boost-their-defenses/2014/07/06/8b2455ca-02e8-11e4-8fd0-3a663dfa68ac_story.html)

921.

Angelina Jolie sold the first pictures of her biological children for a total of $23.7 million dollars. She donated it all to charity.

Reference:
(http://en.wikipedia.org/w/index.php?title=Angelina_Jolie)

922.

Nobody knows the release date of Super Mario Bros. in the United States.

Reference: (http://www.theverge.com/2015/9/14/9324833/super-mario-brothers-30th-anniversary-date)

923.

As part of their animal welfare measures, the Nazis banned vivisection of animals and commercial trapping, and severely restricted hunting, shoeing of horses, and boiling live lobsters.

Reference:(http://en.wikipedia.org/w/index.php?title=Animal_welfare_in_Nazi_Germany&oldid=476576818#Measures)

924.

After the Battle of New Orleans during the War of 1812, 500 British soldiers that were pretending to be dead rose up and surrendered themselves to the victorious Americans.

Reference:
(https://en.wikipedia.org/wiki/Battle_of_New_Orleans#Battle_of_January_8)

925.

A man lived in a French airport departure lounge for 17 years. He entered the airport and "lost" his passport. As he had no passport he could not fly to his destination, the U.K., but he had entered France legally so he could not be expelled.

Reference: (http://en.wikipedia.org/wiki/Mehran_Karimi_Nasseri)

926.

Grover Cleveland was on the cover of the $20 bill before being replaced by Andrew Jackson in 1928.

Reference: (https://en.wikipedia.org/wiki/United_States_twenty-dollar_bill)

927.

Dallas Horton is an Oklahoma man who shot police officers as they breached his residence after a prank call citing that he had planted a bomb at a preschool.

Reference: (http://www.foxnews.com/us/2015/01/19/oklahoma-man-at-center-police-shooting-said-never-made-11-call-that-led-to-raid/)

928.

"The Girl" from Ipanema is the second most recorded pop song after "Yesterday" by the Beatles.

Reference: (https://wikipedia.org/wiki/The_Girl_from_Ipanema)

929.

Rabies are not only mentioned in Homer's writings, but they're also the most likely origin of vampire and zombie folklore.

Reference: (http://www.theverge.com/2013/4/18/4201878/sick-idea-how-rabies-spawned-vampires-and-zombies)

930.

The computer used to generate the CGI scenes in "Tron" had 2 megabytes of memory and a maximum storage capacity of 330 megabytes.

Reference: (https://en.wikipedia.org/wiki/Tron#Pre-production)

931.

Bill Gates has donated over $28 billion to charity and has stated that he wishes to donate a further 95% of his wealth.

Reference: (http://en.wikipedia.org/w/index.php?title=Bill_Gates)

932.

There is a fruit that has been described as the "King of the Fruits" and as having an odor of "pig shit, turpentine and onions, garnished with a gym sock." It can be smelled from yards away and is forbidden from local hotels, subways, airports and public transportation throughout Southeast Asia.

Reference: (http://www.xojane.com/healthy/giving-the-gift-of-durianthe-garlicky-garbage-fruit)

933.

More people die from prescription painkiller overdoses than from heroin and cocaine overdoses combined.

Reference:
(http://www.cdc.gov/features/vitalsigns/PainkillerOverdoses/)

934.

Thomas Francis Meagher designed Ireland's flag. He was sentenced to life in the prison colony of Tasmania by the British, only to escape to the United States, where he became a General in the Union Army during the Civil War, and eventually the territorial Governor of Montana.

Reference:
(https://en.wikipedia.org/wiki/Thomas_Francis_Meagher)

935.

A cabbie told Bill Murray that he was frustrated that he drove 14 hours a day and didn't have enough time to practice playing his saxophone. So Bill Murray drove the cab while the cabbie sat in the back and practiced.

Reference: (http://pagesix.com/2014/09/05/bill-murray-drove-a-taxi-while-the-cabbie-played-his-sax-in-the-back/)

936.

The sirens of Greek Mythology were a mix of a woman and a bird.

Reference: (http://www.ancient.eu/Siren/)

937.

In 1988, a contestant on the game show "Super Password" won the highest jackpot in the history of the show at the time, which was $55,000, only to be arrested shortly after due to a viewer of the show revealing that the contestant was a wanted fraudster in Alaska, Indiana, and California.

Reference:(https://en.wikipedia.org/wiki/Password_Plus_and_Super_Password#Kerry_Ketchem)

938.

Yacouba Sawadogo is known as the man who stopped the desert, using a farming technique called Zai.

Reference: (https://www.youtube.com/watch?v=9_35VAA7it4)

939.

North Korea and South Korea are still technically in a state of war and have been since 1950.

Reference: (http://www.businessinsider.com/ap-rival-koreas-trade-artillery-fire-at-border-over-broadcasts-2015-8?utm_source=feedly&utm_medium=webfeeds)

940.

The longest film ever is 30 days long and has a 7 hour and 20 minute trailer.

Reference: (https://thefilmstage.com/trailer/the-longest-film-ever-made-receives-7-hour-and-20-minute-trailer/)

941.

An American psychologist at the University of Wisconsin developed an insane experiment called the "Pit of Despair", which involved socially isolating young monkeys for up to a year at a time. The monkeys developed psychosis, would cannibalize their offspring and commit suicide.

Reference:
(http://en.wikipedia.org/wiki/Pit_of_despair#Background)

942.

In 2004, the notorious South American gang MS-13 organized for a bus full of civilians to be shot to death in a protest against the Honduran Government reinstating the death penalty.

Reference: (https://en.wikipedia.org/wiki/MS-13#Publicized_crimes)

943.

A woman lived in a man's house for almost a year undetected, during this time she stole food and water, and used his shower. She was finally caught after the owner installed video cameras.

Reference:
(http://www.telegraph.co.uk/news/newstopics/howaboutthat/2054057/Homeless-woman-comes-out-of-closet.html)

944.

An entire village was built on the coast of Malta for the 1980s "Popeye" movie.

Reference: (https://en.wikipedia.org/wiki/Popeye_Village)

945.

MTV banned Beavis and Butthead from referencing fire, specifically Beavis' "Fire" chant, after an arson was blamed on the show. In response, the show had Beavis chant words similar to fire such as fryer. The ban was lifted for the revival and Beavis says fire 7 times in the first video segment.

Reference: (http://en.wikipedia.org/wiki/Beavis_and_Butt-head)

946.

President Ronald Regan honored the crew of NASA's Challenger tragedy by postponing the 1986 State of the Union, to deliver one of the most significant speeches of the 20th century.

Reference:
(https://en.wikipedia.org/wiki/Space_Shuttle_Challenger_disaster#Aftermath)

947.

While living in China, a 10 year old Kanye West would breakdance for other students in exchange for sheep meat skewers.

Reference: (http://www.complex.com/music/2013/02/50-things-you-didnt-know-about-kanye-west/mj-dancing)

948.

In 320 BC, a Greek poet named Archestratus was the first person in history to write a cookbook.

Reference: (https://en.wikipedia.org/wiki/Archestratus)

949.

The World Trade Center site in New York City was the longest burning structural fire in history.

Reference: (https://www.newscientist.com/article/dn1634-ground-zeros-fires-still-burning/)

950.

A study involving college students in the United States and Germany found that people who show hostility towards gay people are more likely to have same-sex desires.

Reference: (http://www.scientificamerican.com/article/homophobes-might-be-hidden-homosexuals/)

951.

There is a Japanese expression, "manaita no ueno koi", meaning "a carp laid on a chopping block". It's used to describe a person who keeps their cool in the face of an imminent and definite danger, and it derives from the carp's uniquely calm disposition when it is about to be cut up.

Reference: (http://english.stackexchange.com/questions/162539/are-there-metaphoric-english-expressions-meaning-keeping-composure-at-a-fatal-m)

952.

Your heart doesn't have pain receptors so if you're having a heart attack, it is the pain receptors in other body areas and not the heart directly that are causing you to feel pain.

Reference: (https://www.healthtap.com/topics/does-the-heart-have-pain-receptors)

953.

If you catch a sturgeon in the UK, it by law, has to be offered to the royal family.

Reference: (http://en.wikipedia.org/wiki/Royal_fish)

954.

The current heir of the Hapsburg family is a Formula 1 driver.

Reference:
(https://en.wikipedia.org/wiki/Ferdinand_Zvonimir_von_Habsburg)

955.

From 2003 to 2008, over $40 billion in cash was flown from the Federal Reserve to Baghdad. Now, nobody knows what happened to the money.

Reference: (http://www.cnbc.com/id/45031100#)

956.

The Shane Company is not a local Seattle jewelry company but is one of the largest jewelry companies in the United States.

Reference: (https://en.wikipedia.org/wiki/Shane_Company)

957.

More than 1,000 experts, including Stephen Hawking, Elon Musk and Steve Wozniak, have signed an open letter urging a global ban on AI weapons systems.

Reference: (http://bgr.com/2015/07/28/stephen-hawking-elon-musk-steve-wozniak-ai-weapons/)

958.

The 10,000 Brunei Dollar Bill is the world's most valuable banknote. A single bill is worth approximately $7,400 USD.

Reference:(https://en.wikipedia.org/wiki/Brunei_dollar#2004.E2.80. 932007_.28polymer.29_series)

959.

During Hurricane Sandy in 2012, Peer 1 Hosting was in danger of its Manhattan data center going offline due to a lack of power. They were able to get 25 people to carry buckets of fuel oil up 17 floors to the backup generators. They managed to stay online the entire time.

Reference: (http://www.informationweek.com/cloud/7-data-center-disasters-youll-never-see-coming/d/d-id/1320702?image_number=5)

960.

The United States cut off diplomatic ties to the Vatican for sending a letter and a signed picture of Pope Pius IX to Jefferson Davis during the Civil War.

Reference:
(https://en.wikipedia.org/wiki/Pope_Pius_IX_and_the_United_States
)

961.

Artist Peter von Tiesenhausen made the top 6 inches of his 800 acre farm a copyrighted work of art to keep oil pipelines out. It costs oil companies $500 per hour to talk to him.

Reference: (http://illahie.blogspot.ca/2014/04/why-art-of-peter-von-tiesenhausen.html)

962.

American Idol's William Hung, who became famous for his off-key rendition of "She Bangs," went on to sell more albums than 3 of the show's winners.

Reference:(https://en.wikipedia.org/wiki/List_of_American_Idol_alumni_album_sales_in_the_United_States)

963.

Shaolin Monks condition their testicles to withstand heavy beatings—the technique is called the "Iron Egg Skill."

Reference: (https://www.youtube.com/watch?v=Js_3bIni52I)

964.

Croatia launched a program called "Fresh Start," which wiped away debt for 60,000 low-income Croatians who have been struggling to pay their bills in an effort to boost consumer confidence and spending. The state agreed to forgive up to $8,830 per individual.

Reference: (http://money.cnn.com/2015/02/03/pf/debt-forgiveness-croatia/)

965.

Conditions seemed so bleak in America during the Great Depression that people in Cameroon sent $3.77 to New York for food relief.

Reference:
(http://www.digitalhistory.uh.edu/disp_textbook.cfm?smtID=2&psid=3434)

966.

Treasury Secretary Alexander Hamilton was the target of an extortion scheme concocted by his mistress and her husband. The affair effectively ended his political career.

Reference: (http://www.smithsonianmag.com/history/alexander-hamiltons-adultery-and-apology-18021947/)

967.

SeaWorld is the largest rescue and rehabilitation program for animals in the world, saving over 24,000 animals, and donating millions of dollars to conservation efforts across the globe.

Reference: (http://www.awesomeocean.com/2014/12/04/four-reasons-condemning-seaworld-really-bad-idea/)

968.

In 1969, 14 black University of Wyoming athletes were thrown off their team for proposing to wear armbands in protest against Brigham Young University's racist policies.

Reference: (http://www.uwyo.edu/ahc/research/topics/black14.html)

969.

Jackey Vinson, the man who played Lucas from the 1989 movie "The Wizard," is a registered sex offender.

Reference: (http://www.homefacts.com/offender-detail/NY20653/Jack-Vinson.html)

970.

In 2012, a Japanese mathematician, Shinichi Mochizuki, presented proof for the "ABC Conjuncture," which is one of the most important, unsolved problems in math. However, the proof is so difficult and abstract, that not even his peers can understand it, so the conjuncture remains unsolved to this day.

Reference: (http://www.nature.com/news/the-biggest-mystery-in-mathematics-shinichi-mochizuki-and-the-impenetrable-proof-1.18509)

971.

Pepsi is now selling as "Pecsi" in Mexico as about one third of Mexicans can't pronounce "Pepsi."

Reference: (http://www.tuvez.com/videos/pepsi-now-selling-as-pecsi-in-mexico/)

972.

When Disney acquired Star Wars, they ensured all their future works would be equal canon with the original movies.

Reference: (https://en.wikipedia.org/wiki/Star_Wars_canon)

973.

Nike made a commercial depicting a Samburu tribesman saying "Just Do It" in his native language. An American anthropologist called them out. The spoken phrase actually meant, "I don't want these, give me big shoes." Nike's response, "We thought nobody in America would know what he said."

Reference: (http://www.nytimes.com/1989/02/15/opinion/topics-of-the-times-if-the-shoe-doesn-t-fit.html)

974.

The Little Mermaid statue has been decapitated twice, had her arm sawn off, has been blown up with explosives and had a dildo stuck to her.

Reference:
(https://en.wikipedia.org/wiki/The_Little_Mermaid_(statue))

975.

The book 'What Every Man Thinks About Apart From Sex' which contained just 200 BLANK pages outsold both Harry Potter & The Da Vinci Code.

Reference: (http://www.amazon.com/Every-Thinks-About-Apart-Inside-ebook/dp/B004NIFSRA/ref=tmm_kin_swatch_0?_encoding=UTF8&sr=&qid=)

976.

The Star Wars creators were very thorough in making sure that all of the Clone Army looked and sounded the same.

Reference: (http://starwars.wikia.com/wiki/Temuera_Morrison)

977.

A Polish midwife, responsible for delivery of over 3,000 children in Auschwitz, marked them with a "tattoo" that would not be recognized by the SS guards, hoping that in the future it would be possible to recover these children.

Reference: (http://www.seattlecatholic.com/article_20050104.html)

978.

"Datum" is the singular form of "data."

Reference: (http://www.dictionary.com/browse/datum?s=t)

979.

South African scientists have discovered that 400 year old tobacco pipes excavated from the garden of William Shakespeare contained cannabis, suggesting the playwright to might have written some of his famous works while high.

Reference:
(http://www.sajs.co.za/sites/default/files/publications/pdf/SAJS%201 11_7-8_Thackeray_Sci%20Corr.pdf)

980.

Men account for 97% of alimony payers.

Reference:
(http://www.forbes.com/sites/emmajohnson/2014/11/20/why-do-so-few-men-get-alimony/#2bb5ac723c29)

981.

Walking Corpse Syndrome is a mental disorder in which patients experience delusions that they are dead, do not exist, are putrefying or have lost their vital organs.

Reference: (http://en.wikipedia.org/wiki/Cotard_delusion)

982.

Predominantly Catholic countries receive more tourists per capita than other predominantly Christian countries.

Reference: (http://www.nationmaster.com/country-info/stats/Economy/Tourist-arrivals/Per-capita)

983.

You can get high from smoking dead scorpions.

Reference: (http://www.dawn.com/news/1252264/smoking-dead-scorpions-is-kps-latest-dangerous-addiction)

984.

A woman was caught making meth inside of a Wal-Mart, while it was open.

Reference: (http://www.fox23.com/news/news/breaking-news/woman-caught-making-meth-inside-s-tulsa-walmart/ndkkT/)

985.

The Queen never gave a press interview, went to an election or publicly expressed a personal opinion.

Reference:
(https://en.wikipedia.org/wiki/Personality_and_image_of_Queen_Elizabeth_II)

986.

Light can echo in space.

Reference: (http://en.wikipedia.org/wiki/Light_echo)

987.

Georgy de Hevesy dissolved 2 Nobel Prize medals to protect them and their owners from the Nazis. He had them recasted by the Nobel Foundation after the war.

Reference:
(http://www.npr.org/sections/krulwich/2011/10/03/140815154/dissolve-my-nobel-prize-fast-a-true-story)

988.

In Hiroshima, there are permanent shadows caused by the intensity of the nuclear blast when the bomb was dropped. Sometimes, there were shadows left of people, but no bodies found. This resulted from the extreme heat of the explosion which vaporized the bodies, leaving the shadows behind. The shadows are a unique occurrence from the nuclear explosion and they remain even after many years.

Reference: (http://www.pcf.city.hiroshima.jp/virtual/cgi-bin/museum.cgi?no=1001&l=e)

989.

There's a movement called the Second Vermont Republic that calls for the secession of Vermont from the United States.

Reference:
(https://en.wikipedia.org/wiki/Second_Vermont_Republic)

990.

The phrase "to turn a blind eye," comes from British Vice Admiral Nelson, who was blind in one eye. In one battle, when he was signaled to stop attacking a fleet of Danish ships, he held up a telescope to his blind eye, saying, "I really do not see the signal," and attacked anyway.

Reference: (https://en.wikipedia.org/wiki/Turning_a_blind_eye)

991.

Compared with a single cigarette, one hookah session delivers approximately 2.5 times the nicotine, 25 times the tar, 125 times the smoke and 10 times the carbon monoxide.

Reference: (http://www.mensfitness.com/life/entertainment/hookah-packs-25-times-tar-single-cigarette)

992.

There are trees in the northeast United States that can bear 40 different kinds of fruit, all on the same tree.

Reference: (en.wikipedia.org/wiki/Tree_of_40_Fruit)

993.

Most pictures that we see of "old" Einstein are many years after he published anything groundbreaking, as his noteworthy achievements are from his miracle year of 1905, when he was 26 years old.

Reference: (https://en.wikipedia.org/wiki/Annus_Mirabilis_papers)

994.

Members of the Westboro Baptist Church have been banned from entering Canada for hate speech.

Reference:
(http://en.wikipedia.org/wiki/Freedom_of_speech#Limitations)

995.

Benedict Arnold was a decorated patriot and even used his own money to pay for supplies and training for soldiers before he became an infamous traitor.

Reference:
(http://www.usnews.com/news/national/articles/2008/06/27/benedict-arnold-a-traitor-but-once-a-patriot)

996.

South Korea has a law against teenagers under 16 playing video games after midnight.

Reference: (http://edition.cnn.com/2011/11/22/world/asia/south-korea-gaming/index.html)

997.

The Indonesian island of Flores has legends of humanoid creatures that were dumb, stole and once kidnapped a child to teach them cooking, before being exterminated. Scientist speculate that these may be folk memories of Homo floresiensis, which were a short hominid who lived on Flores until 13,000 years ago.

Reference: (https://en.wikipedia.org/wiki/Ebu_gogo)

998.

Thousands of lions are being bred on farms to be shot by wealthy foreign trophy hunters.

Reference:
(http://www.theguardian.com/environment/2013/jun/03/canned-hunting-lions-bred-slaughter)

999.

The Black Death was first introduced to Europe in Crimea after the Mongol Army catapulted infected corpses over city walls.

Reference:
(https://en.wikipedia.org/wiki/Black_Death#European_outbreak)

1000.

A mysterious lake that is 10 to 18 meters deep appeared in a drought stricken area in southern Tunisia overnight.

Reference: (http://www.ibtimes.co.uk/gafsa-beach-mysterious-lake-discovered-drought-stricken-tunisia-could-be-radioactive-1459288)